THE SPORTS NUTRITION HANDBOOK

TEN STEPS

TO A LEANER BODY, LESS ILLNESS AND GREATER ATHLETIC PERFORMANCE

Steven D. Spainhower, M.S., D.C., L.M.S.N.

*Edited by Amanda Carlson, M.S., R.D.
and Jeff Kotterman, B.S., L.M.S.N.*

Education Resources

The information contained in this book is based upon the research and personal and professional experiences of the author and editors. The material is not intended as a substitute for consulting with a physician or other healthcare provider. The publisher and authors believe the information in this book should be available to the public. The publisher and authors are not responsible for any adverse effects or consequences resulting from the use of the suggestions, preparation, or procedures discussed in this book.

Education Resources, L.L.C.
1260 N. 1280 West
St. George, UT 84770
435.313.1271

ISBN: 0-9637573-2-6

AUTHOR:

Steven D. Spainhower, M.S., D.C., L.S.N.
Dr. Spainhower is a chiropractic physician, specializing in exercise and clinical nutrition. He holds a Master's Degree in exercise science, is a licensed sports nutritionist, and has worked with athletes of all ages. Dr. Spainhower is available for speaking engagements.

Please direct comments and inquiries to:
stevenspainhower@gmail.com

EDITORS:

Amanda Carlson, M.S., R.D.
Ms. Carlson holds two Master's Degrees from Florida State University—one in exercise physiology and one in sports nutrition. She is a registered dietician. Ms. Carlson works with professional athletes in Phoenix, Arizona.

Jeff Kotterman, B.S., L.M.S.N.
Mr. Kotterman is the director of the National Association of Sports Nutrition in San Diego, California. He is a licensed master sports nutritionist.

Book and cover design by Kent Bingham, Ogden, Utah.

Many great people have helped me with this work. My wife, Linda, and our children—Stephanie, Andrew, Audrey, Elise, and Moriah—have supported and inspired me. The gracious Dr. Dan Benardot gave permission to include anecdotes from his personal experiences with athletes. He is a real leader. I also am grateful for input from excellent athletes like Derek McAllister.

CONTENTS

Contents

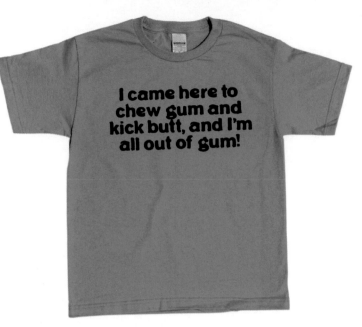

Introduction

At a festival on the day before the St. George City Marathon, I noticed some entertaining T-shirt messages. One read, "I came here to chew gum and kick butt, and I'm all out of gum!" It put a smile on my face, and I realized that while a few runners came to win, the vast majority came to participate, to do their best, and to celebrate the spirit of accomplishment. Whether you're a serious student athlete or a fitness-minded adult, this handbook is for you.

The benefits of heart and muscular fitness are widely known. Millions of us are hitting the gyms, the streets or equipment at home. We want to live a higher quality of life, to feel and look good, perhaps compete better, love better, and live longer. Trainers and coaches teach us how to do aerobic exercise, lift weights and stretch. We practice the skills of our favorite sports. Yet, many are frustrated with mediocre results. Why?

Is it genetics? Partly. Is it desire and intensity? Partly. Studies tell us that the difference between average and excellent results is the right nutrition. It's too often the "missing link." Knowing what to eat and when to eat can blast you forward like you've never experienced. Without proper athletic nutrition, it's like planting a garden and weeding it, but never watering it. It's a waste of time. Your hard work in the gym is of little value without the optimal timing of foods, fluids and supplements.

Whatever type of athlete you consider yourself to be, the benefits of smart sports nutrition are clear: personal best performances, greater strength, more energy, lower body fat, less illness, and quick recovery. This handbook is dedicated to those who want to be "leaner and meaner." The elite athletes know that effective sports nutrition makes the difference between 4th quarter drop-outs and 4th quarter butt kickers. Without the right fuel for your training, you are like a car with cheap fuel, flat tires, or no water in the radiator.

As I've talked with athletes of all ages, I have found that some of them think they know what's good for them already. To some degree, they are right, especially regarding food preferences. But sadly, they miss critical points of sports nutrition that would not only make workouts more enjoyable, but also prevent muscle wasting and illness. One guy told me he didn't really care about all that. Well, that's his choice.

If you're reading this, you might be one of the people branded with "Student-Athlete" on your forehead. It's not all bad though. In fact, people envy you. Many of you get scholarship money to play a sport while getting an education. People admire your skills, strength, speed, stamina, and yes, your courage.

The gymnastics team of a well-known university recently experienced near tragedy because of faulty sports nutrition counseling. The strength coach had jumped on the high-protein-diet "bandwagon" and was excited to try it out with the gymnastics team. (Indeed, these diets help people to lose weight, but they cause problems for serious athletes.) After a few days on the new diet, the athletes began to notice less energy and stamina during workouts. They fatigued early and felt weak during routines.

It became obvious that the new diet had hurt their performance. Two athletes were diagnosed with "overtraining syndrome" and had to quit competing. After three weeks of the high protein diet, the strength coach took some "serious heat," and the team returned to a more proven sports diet with higher carbohydrate. The athletes quickly regained their normal strength and endurance.

As you read this handbook, please keep in mind that each statement comes from analyzing a great deal of information. Lengthy explanations would defeat the purpose of the book: to save you time and provide you with the bottom lines of scientific research so you can make educated decisions. Short and to the point is the goal. **When research is cited, the author's name is stated in parenthesis.** You can find the full references of peer-reviewed journals and books at the back of the handbook, listed alphabetically by author's name.

The Sports Nutrition Handbook works for the following reasons: 1) Most people would rather read a summary of the best research than push through ten books to find it; 2) It can go with you all day like a planner, remind you of your goals, be a quick ready reference, and help you track your progress; 3) It simplifies the research on over 50 supplements so you can safely benefit; 4) And hopefully, because it will help motivate you to reach your athletic potential!

For student athletes, strength training occurs at a specified time and place; therefore, a strength and conditioning coach can influence athletes tremendously with on-site supervision. Athletic training also takes place at a facility with hands-on work. If you miss a session, someone gets after you. However, applying lifestyle strategies requires a 24-hour commitment from the athlete. A tangible handbook (or a dedicated roommate) may be the best way to reinforce what are arguably the most important ingredients in sports science—eating, drinking, supplementing and sleeping right. The strength trainers and athletic trainers don't go home with you. This handbook does.

There are some excellent books on sports nutrition, but most people don't have the time or desire to read the scientific literature. And unless you're a nutrition or physiology major, it is often difficult to understand. It's extremely valuable to have a "bottom-line" summary of the literature so you can make sense about what is right for you.

Among the problems in the world of athletics, the health of student-athletes is perhaps our biggest crisis. Injuries, eating disorders, steroid abuse, and death are just a few of the critical problems related to nutrition. Congressional hearings search for answers to this epidemic. The pressure to win, combined with the lack of accurate, clear, and usable information leads young athletes to making decisions that could jeopardize their performance, their health, and sometimes their life. The hype in supplement advertisements—"Blast those biceps!" "Turn your chest into a fortress!"—only encourage supplement abuse with words of fantasy. They have little regard for the mortality and actual physiology of the human body.

Some of the well-budgeted universities have hired a full-time staff sports nutritionist, and I applaud them! Most schools, however, rely on trainers and coaches who, though well-meaning, are typically not qualified as dieticians. Advice is given at the athlete's request, merely scratching the surface of what is needed. Mental and physical illness from the misuse of supplements is common. Many athletes, especially females, struggle with eating disorders and are embarrassed to visit the staff nutritionist because of the associated stigma and reputation that follows. Even with a staff nutritionist, accessibility and time are limited; whereas an athlete can refer to the handbook in their possession at any time.

This handbook is not intended to diagnose disease or prescribe medicine. It educates and helps the reader make informed choices and determine whether they should seek advice from a physician. The handbook does not intend to promote any single brand of products.

Notes to Trainers and Coaches

An effective recruiting tool for a college is an emphasis on proper sports nutrition. Parents love to hear that their child will receive a research-based handbook and be guided in proper sports nutrition. Recruiters can sincerely explain that the athletic department they represent emphasizes safe, sound, and legal nutritional practices.

To reinforce the concepts your athletes/clients are reading, you should be thoroughly familiar with this handbook. Your influence can be very powerful, especially with regard to healthy attitudes, such as those surrounding body composition. Trainers and coaches should insure that measurements of body composition are done privately and confidentially, in case the athlete does not wish others to hear the results and is shy about asking for privacy. If significant changes are noted, explore and explain to the athlete how and why those changes took place rather than merely reporting the change. Keep in mind the homeostatic mechanisms of individuals. Genetics determine limits of body fat changes. For example, ten percent body fat is feasible for some males, but not for others.

Body fat measurements should be taken with the same technique and examiner each time. Keep track of changes through the annual training cycles. During the off-season, an athlete should not increase by more than four percent. Measurements of body fat should occur only two to four times a year. More often can create fear and discouragement. Daily weigh-ins are discouraged. Body fat percentage is a more accurate determiner of athletic readiness than total body weight is.

Coaches and trainers who make irrational weight loss demands cause athletes to use illegal or unsafe tactics to burn fat. This increases the risk for law suits. It is imperative to realize the differences in body types and genetic body fat thermostats. Encourage strength, energy, and flexibility, more than body weight. Student athletes have enough sources of emotional stress—studies, family, social life, money—without pouring on body composition expectations. The school or clinic should establish a policy for responding to coaches, trainers, teachers, and other institutional staff who make inappropriate remarks to athletes.

The Short Version: The Top 30 Tips

L et's cut to the chase. Many athletes don't want to read a lot of explanation and background information on the science of sports nutrition. This section is for them. It contains the "Top 30" bottom-line points from thousands of pages of scientific literature. If you read and "digest" (pun intended) the following key points, you'll know the "nitty gritty" of what is taught in the best textbooks. For athletes, coaches, and trainers who want to understand these concepts more fully, you can refer to the pages noted after each item. The more of these items you adopt into your lifestyle, the better athlete you can become.

1 **Fiber is filling.** For example, apples help people to manage body fat by curbing appetite with pectin, one of the best types of fiber. The fiber is filling and helps to move food through the intestines, slowing the rate of carbohydrate absorption into the bloodstream, which helps to stabilize blood sugar, curb hunger, and minimize fat storage. Eat one or two per day with your tuna or turkey sandwich. *For more info, see pages 76-78.*

2 **Six smaller meals a day are more effective at building muscle and reducing fat than three larger meals.** Eating frequently fuels muscles and minimizes fat storage. And it starts with breakfast! Breakfast gives you energy and makes it easier to get six meals in a day. Use an insulated drink bottle as a "portable refrigerator" to keep your meal replacement shake cold all day, and pack a good energy bar for one meal per day. **At least four meals a day should consist of real food.** If sticking to six balanced meals per day is difficult for you, start with five, and choose one splurge day per week to eat whatever you want. That should make it psychologically easier to follow your nutrition plan the other days. If you've got the six meals a day under control, you'll probably be able to do the next step: adjusting your calories down about 20% **on days of inactivity.** Reduce your intake of carbohydrates and fats on inactive days; stay with the same amount of protein. *For more info, see pages 38-40.*

3 You have a 30- to 45-minute nutritional window of opportunity after exercise to kick-start recovery, speed up the reconstruction of glycogen in muscles, decrease the damaging effects of the hormone cortisol, and start protein synthesis for maximal muscle building.** Use a drink with a ratio of 3:1 or 4:1—fast acting carbohydrates to whey protein. Include one gram of glutamine and leucine, Vitamin C (250mg) and Vitamin E (200 IU). *For more info, see pages 73-75.*

4 Public places are famous for collecting and sharing infectious germs. Wash your hands often, and sleep an average of nine hours per night (if you're a teen or young adult) to strengthen your immune system and to maximize muscle growth. **Keep a regular routine as much as you can.** On the night before a big event, sleep your normal hours. If you are used to eight hours of sleep, starting at 10:30, stay with that. On game day, eat foods you are accustomed to. *For more info, see pages 71-73.*

5 **If you are over age 40 and diagnosed with insulin resistance, you should consider a daily nutrient ratio of 50/20/30:** 50% from carbohydrates, 20% from fats and 30% from protein—especially if your body fat is above 20% and you are male, or if your bodyfat is above 28% and you are female. *For more info, see pages 31-34.*

6 **Avoid stomach and intestinal problems by getting fiber and plenty of water every day.** Athletes who drink three high protein/low carb shakes a day often get constipated, may not store enough muscle glycogen for the next day's workout, may experience kidney damage, and sometimes get bad flatulence from intolerance to a particular type of protein. *For more info, see pages 45-47.*

7 **Whey protein gets into the bloodstream faster than other sources of protein, such as casein, soy, egg, and meat.** It works during and soon after workouts. For meals other than during and after workouts, eat the other protein types, such as soy milk, eggs, beans, turkey, tuna and lean beef, along with lots of vegetables, fruits and whole grains. *For more info, see pages 45-47 and 73-75.*

8 **Use some of the supplements that are A graded** in this handbook, proven safe and effective for your sport. *For more info, see pages 57-68.*

9 **Pre-game meals should be high in carbohydrate, moderate in protein, and low in fat.** They should occur three to four hours before competition. If you have a morning event, eat a smaller meal 1½ to 2 hours before competition, then sip a sports drink until the event. Urine that is pale yellow to clear-ish means you are well hydrated. *For more info, see pages 99, 100.*

 Refer to the chart below to determine the proper distribution of nutrients based on your sport-type and gender. *For more info, see pages 28-34.*

Bodybuilder (male)		
50% carbohydrates	25% fats	25% proteins

Bodybuilder (female)		
55% carbohydrates	25% fats	20% proteins

Power Athlete (football, softball, gymnastics, sprinting, etc.)		
55% carbohydrates	25% fats	20% proteins

Strength/Endurance Athlete (basketball, soccer, 400-800m etc.)		
60% carbohydrates	25% fats	15% proteins

Endurance/Distance Athlete		
65-70% carbohydrates	20% fats	15% proteins

11 Water! It builds cells, strengthens muscle (70% of muscle mass is water), protects the brain and spinal cord, controls the balance of electrolytes, and makes blood plasma for carrying oxygen and nutrients to cells. **You should drink water continually.** Most sports drinks are OK, but some are not ideal. Those with about 15g of carbohydrate, 70-150 mg of sodium, 35-60 mg chloride, 50-100 mg potassium, and 75-300 mg magnesium per 8 oz serving (one cup) tend to work best. *(Gisolfi, Coyle, Maughan, Murray)*

When sweating heavily, drink as much and as often as you can stand. Drink before you're thirsty! The general rule is one cup of sports beverage every 10 to 15 minutes during exercise. During and right after exercise, a sports drink with whey protein works better than one without protein. You can add about 15 grams of plain or vanilla whey protein to a quart of sports beverage, and shake it up. Doesn't sound tasty? Most athletes are surprised at how good it tastes (except with the lemonade flavors). *For more info, see pages 50-52.*

12 **Consume less than one gram (.7g to .8g) of protein per pound of body weight per day.** More than that is converted to blood sugar and fat. Excess protein increases urinary output, so it tends to promote dehydration. It takes about five days for protein to become stored energy as glycogen, whereas carbohydrate takes only one to two days. *For more info, see pages 45-47.*

13 **Eating a variety of real foods is the best way to get the vitamins, minerals, carbohydrates, and amino acids you need.** Whole grains, plant oils, vegetables, fruits, fish, chicken, turkey, nuts, beans, and eggs are the most important foods. Find a multi-vitamin and mineral supplement—it doesn't have to be expensive—with low doses, less than the RDA's of each, as insurance on days that you don't eat a fortified cereal. *For more info, see pages 18,19.*

14 When traveling, take your favorite energy/protein bars and perhaps a can of tuna in your travel bag, in case your sports foods are difficult to locate. Keep in mind that energy bars with more than five grams of fiber can work like a laxative on the digestive tract. If you eat high fiber before exercise, don't run far from a toilet. *For more info, see page 93.*

15 Start your day with the right nutrients! Whole grain cereal with milk and a cup of fruit juice is a good breakfast for a smaller, endurance athlete. If the cereal is fortified with vitamins and minerals, such as Total or Product 19, skip your multivitamin pill that day. Oatmeal, eggs, and fruit would make an excellent breakfast, especially for power athletes. *For more info, see pages 40, 41.*

16 Excessive exercise and/or not eating enough are the common causes of menstrual problems in female athletes. Females, especially distance runners, need to supplement with iron, eat their required calories, and consume foods that contain folic acid. *For more info, see pages 52, 55, 58.*

17 Take charge of yourself. Only you can be responsible for your success. Top-performing athletes study when it's time to study, exercise when it's time to exercise, hang-out when it's time to hang-out, eat when it's time to eat, and sleep when it's time to sleep! *For more info, see pages 70-72.*

18 **To gain one pound of muscle per week**, lift weights two to three times a week, eat 500 to 1000 more calories per day than your normal caloric needs as figured in the section on "Personal Caloric Calculator," and sleep an average of nine hours per night. *For more info, see pages 70-77.*

19 **To lose one pound of fat per week**, exercise intensely, eat six meals a day, and eat 500 to 1000 fewer calories per day than your normal caloric needs as figured in the section on "Personal Caloric Calculator." *For more info, see pages 70-77.*

20 BCAA's (branched-chain amino acids), such as valine, leucine, and isoleucine, are a major part of muscle tissue. They are broken down during exercise to provide energy. Leucine gets oxidized and used up first, and without it, you can't make new muscle protein, **so it's a good idea to add one gram of leucine, along with one gram of glutamine, to your recovery drink.** 25% of whey protein is BCAA's. (Glutamine can help to prevent illness.) *For more info, see page 61, 62.*

21 The timing and content of meals are very important. **Eating every 2½ hours works well for most people.** During the 24 hours after weight lifting, be sure to eat well, which means getting your quota of proteins and carbs so the muscles can rebuild optimally. Also, fast digesting (high glycemic) carbs should be consumed after workouts to start recovery quickly. Slow (low glycemic) carbs should be eaten for later meals. *For more info, see pages 40-42, 73-75, 120.*

22 Free radicals in the body, caused by exercise and other things, create oxidative stress, damage cells, mitochondria, and break down proteins. **Supplement your diet with Vitamins C (250 to 750mg/day) and E (200 to 400 IU/day) to combat free radicals.** *For more info, see page 60-62.*

23 If you weigh approximately 200 hundred pounds, you can probably tolerate up to 60 grams of carbohydrate (that's 4 cups of sports drink) consumed during one hour of exercise; half that much if you're 100 pounds. *(Bernadot)*

24 **Glycogen is the most important source of energy for athletes. Glycogen is chains of glucose (blood sugar) stored in muscles and in the liver.** When it runs out, you're in trouble. That's why athletes who workout daily must eat a high carbohydrate diet, eg. 60% of calories from carbs. The longer and slower you exercise, the more protein and fat you burn. So, an hour of jogging will shrink your muscles and body fat. Body builders do very little cardio/aerobic training. *For more info, see pages 95-97.*

25 **The longer you go without eating, the more your body breaks down muscles for energy, and the more you tend to store fat when you finally eat again.** When you are not huffing and puffing with hard exercise, you have plenty of oxygen in your cells. Fat and protein are used for energy (ATP) when plenty of oxygen is present. *For more info, see pages 95-97.*

26 Intense workouts trigger an inflammatory response from slight damage to the muscle cells. The muscles get "pumped" with blood flow to bring in oxygen, nutrients, and inflammatory chemicals, then

blood carries away the waste products. This blood flow stimulates healing, growth, and strength. If you can increase blood flow the next day without overworking the muscle, great! The risk is working the muscle too hard, too soon, which breaks down cells again, not allowing growth. So, a few push-ups, or a short, intense cardio session the day after a workout is enough to increase blood flow to upper body muscles. **Never put the same muscles through strenuous weight lifting two days in a row.** *For more info, see pages 73-76.*

27 **Learn how to estimate how many grams and calories are in your meals.** Start with the serving of protein. One small chicken breast contains about 30 grams, one cup of cottage cheese contains about 25 grams, 4 ounces of meat or fish contains about 28 grams, one cup of soy milk has about 7 grams, a slice of whole wheat bread provides about 5 grams. If your nutrient ratio is 60/25/15, and you need 30 grams of protein per meal, then the carbs on your plate should weigh 4 times more than the protein. *For more info, see pages 121-123, 129, 138, 139.*

28 **Eating well doesn't have to be expensive.** Check the grocery ads from the newspaper (usually Sundays), and buy what's on sale at a reduced price. The "gotta havits" for many athletes are the following: peanut butter, whole wheat bread, oatmeal, frozen vegetables, apples, oranges, bananas, frozen chicken breasts, turkey lunch meat, yogurt, beans, tuna fish, carrot sticks, olive oil (some prefer light-tasting olive oil for cooking), eggs, cottage cheese, soy milk, and whole grain cereal. If you keep these foods in your cupboard and refrigerator, you are set.

29 Visit the following web sites for nutritional information on various fast foods:

www.mcdonalds.com
www.burgerking.com
www.dominoes.com
www.kfc.com
www.tacobell.com
www.dunkindonuts.com

30 Get a stainless steel, insulated drink bottle for your workout drink or meal substitute. (The glass ones can break when dropped.) It's like a portable refrigerator and works well on a busy day. If it's a high-protein, meal replacement drink, mix it with cereal like oatmeal, Grape Nuts or wheat flakes to provide the carbs and fiber you need. Fruit or peanut butter can also add carbs while enhancing the flavor.

STEP 1
Check Your Attitudes at the Door

Ten Steps to Athletic Power

STEP 1:
Check Your Attitudes at the Door

GET REAL ABOUT YOURSELF AND YOUR HANG-UPS

You can't achieve goals without knowing where you are now, mentally and physically. Once you identify "where your head is," as well as your physique, you can set smart goals.

Take a look at the picture below. What do you see?

Now, turn the page and look at the same picture from a different view.

A different perspective can bring more reality into what you think. It's called a paradigm shift.

If you want to excel, you must know your faulty paradigms, your hang-ups about sports nutrition. Sometimes you have to "change your seat" to see something a different way, to get a more accurate viewpoint. This section requires some real maturity because it asks you to see yourself how others might see you. Would people who know you say that you believe in a magic pill or potion, that you are gullible to any product someone recommends, or are you conservative and rely on "three square meals" a day? Would your friends say you are teachable, level-headed, and would like to apply some smart strategies to make yourself better? Where would you put yourself on the sports nutrition attitudes continuum? Are you at either extreme? Peter Pillpopper or Sally Square Meal? Or, are you somewhere in the middle?

Peter Pillpopper

just can't believe that real food is more effective than supplements at building muscle and athletic endurance. He looks for shortcuts to excellence, which don't exist. His urine is an expensive shade of neon yellow, filled with unused supplements. He sees his money swirling down the drain, while getting frustrated at his lack of progress and frequent upset stomach.

Sally Square Meal

is very traditional, buying into the old adage, "three square meals a day," without knowing it sprang from the history of meals in the military, which were served on square plates. It has nothing to do with sports nutritional science. She is reluctant to accept that eating often actually helps her to control her weight and enhances muscle growth, so she continues to struggle with fat gain and hunger.

Scott Sensible

is ready to listen to science and common sense. He is teachable and wants good information. He carries a variety of food in his backpack so he can get six meals a day, though it takes an extra moment of morning preparation. He carefully analyzes information on supplements and tries two or three "A grade supplements" that apply to his sport. He eats more vegetables, even some he hasn't tried for years. He knows that intense workouts are useless if he doesn't fuel his muscles with a variety of real foods. He is dedicated to success, feels energy all day, and sees real progress.

Sports Nutrition Attitudes Continuum

PETER PILLPOPPER	SCOTT SENSIBLE	SALLY SQUARE MEAL

On the Continuum above, mark the line where you honestly see yourself right now.

My Hangups: _____

_____

_____

_____

_____

_____

_____

Now, write at least two of your hang-ups in the space provided. For example, you might write, "I don't eat breakfast." or, "I'm too fat, and ephedrine works the best." Next, decide to look at your hang-ups in a new way, and if necessary, hang them up someplace where you can inspect them for possible flaws. Now you are ready to see what science has to say about your hang-ups, so you can decide if your paradigms need adjusting. **How good or how fit do you want to be?**

One great thing about humans is that they form strong opinions about what is real, not real, good and bad, cool, not cool, what they like, don't like, etc. On the other hand, one lousy thing about humans that they form strong opinions about what is real, not real, good and bad, etc. You see, being stubborn and unwilling to "change your seat," and look at things differently can keep you in the dark and hurt your performance. Understanding other viewpoints can help you not only to grow and make informed decisions, but also can bring more truth, reality, and athletic power into your life.

STEP 2
Know Your Metabolism

STEP 2:
Know Your Metabolism

PERSONAL CALORIC CALCULATOR

Knowing your own metabolism can help you take charge of your nutritional plan for achieving your body and performance goals. Start with the following easy steps. (A calculator is helpful here.)

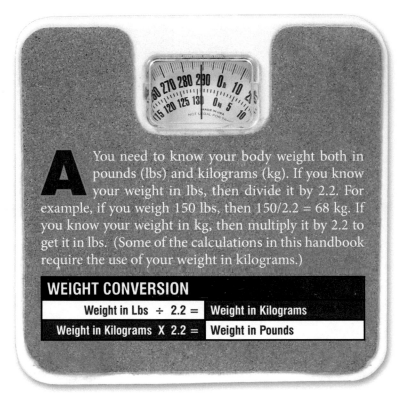

A You need to know your body weight both in pounds (lbs) and kilograms (kg). If you know your weight in lbs, then divide it by 2.2. For example, if you weigh 150 lbs, then 150/2.2 = 68 kg. If you know your weight in kg, then multiply it by 2.2 to get it in lbs. (Some of the calculations in this handbook require the use of your weight in kilograms.)

WEIGHT CONVERSION

Weight in Lbs ÷ 2.2 =	Weight in Kilograms
Weight in Kilograms X 2.2 =	Weight in Pounds

Please write your total body weight in lbs and kg here:

LBS	**Kg**

B Choose one of the following options to determine your daily Resting Energy Expenditure (REE). This is the amount of calories it takes to keep you breathing, thinking, and your heart beating each day.

Males, Ages 18 to 30	
15.3 X body weight in kg + 679 =	
Males, Ages 31 to 60	
11.6 X body weight in kg + 879 =	

Females, Ages 18 to 30	
14.7 X body weight in kg + 496 =	
Females, Ages 31 to 60	
8.7 X body weight in kg + 829 =	

Please round your REE up or down to get rid of any decimal.

Note: Athletes who move from a harsh climate to a milder climate will experience a reduction in their resting energy expenditure. If this applies to you in the last two weeks, reduce your REE by 5%. An easy way to do this is to multiply your REE by .95.

C Figure the calories you use in normal daily activity (NDA) by multiplying a certain percentage by your REE. If you are sedentary (sit most of the day), use 20% to 40% of your REE. If you are moderately active (walk from

class to class for a few hours), use 50% (.50) of your REE. If you are active, (walk a few blocks to and from school, and move around a lot at home or work), use 60% to 80% of your REE.

Your REE from above	Activity Level	NDA calories
X	(Ex: .60) =	

 Next, figure the calories you burn in purposeful exercise (PEC). Find what matches you best from the chart on pages 132-137. (If your chart is missing, use 600 calories if you work out hard for about an hour each day.)

For example, if you weigh 200 lbs and play intense basketball for 40 minutes on a given day, you would multiply 13.2 (calories from the chart) by 40 min. to get the approximate number of calories you burn in that activity. Remember that even though your practices might last over two hours, you need to figure how many minutes you are actually working out hard. There are breaks and standing around at most practices.

Add the three types of caloric expenditure to get your total daily energy expenditure (TDEE). (The effect of eating food on your metabolism is about 5% and is built into the above steps.)

Add them all up	
REE	
+ NDA	
+ PEC	
=	Total (TDEE)

You have just figured your Total Daily Energy Expenditure (TDEE) in calories. This is the number of calories you need to consume to support a day in your life, as you have described, and maintain your weight. Memorize the number. You will need it a bit later. Before going on to nutrients, you should complete the following questionnaire on insulin resistance. It may affect your nutritional plan.

INSULIN RESISTANCE QUESTIONNAIRE

The following self-test will help determine whether you have insulin resistance in some degree. Over one third of the US population suffers from this condition, often called "Syndrome X." It is a major cause of obesity, as well as diabetes and heart disease; however, it can be controlled quite well through an adjusted diet and exercise.

Please check any of the following items that you have now or have ever had. (Some items require a blood test.):

☐ Family history of diabetes, overweight problems, abnormal cholesterol or triglycerides, heart disease, or stroke.

☐ Frequent cravings for sweet or salty, crunchy snack food.

☐ High uric acid or gouty arthritis.

☐ HDL cholesterol lower than 35 mg/dl.

☐ Type 2 diabetes, borderline diabetes, or abnormal glucose tolerance tests—even just during pregnancy.

☐ A difficult time losing weight even if you exercise or cut back on your food intake.

☐ LDL cholesterol higher than 130 mg/dl.

☐ Hypoglycemia

☐ Jitteriness, difficulty thinking, headaches, or nausea that goes away when you eat.

☐ Skin tags (small, painless, flappy skin growths) on your neck, chest, breasts, groin area, or underarms.

☐ A history of irregular menstrual periods, especially skipping months.

☐ High blood pressure, even during pregnancy.

☐ Native-American, Asian, African-American, or Hispanic ancestry.

Write the number of how many items you checked on the insulin resistance questionnaire here: ☐☐☐☐☐☐☐☐☐☐ You will need to refer to it later.

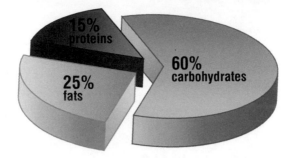

Standard Nutrient Breakdown for Athletes

In this section, you will find out how much of carbohydrate, protein, and fat you should eat each day. For example, some people think they should eat twice as much carbohydrate as they eat protein. Others believe that their sport dictates what the distribution of nutrients should be. Your sport, body fat, size, and biochemistry all help determine your nutrient breakdown. Contrary to what you might think, endurance athletes may need as much protein in their diet as power athletes need. *(Ivy, Portman)* Over prolonged exercise, up to 15% of the burned fuel comes from muscle protein. *(Lemon)* That's one reason why distance runners are less muscular than baseball or football players. Your distribution or ratio of nutrients per meal is crucial to your success as an athlete. Start with a breakdown of 60/25/15. *(Benardot, Burke, Williams, Lemon)* This means that 60% of your TDEE (daily calories) should come from carbohydrates,

25% from fats, and 15% from proteins. This can be adjusted to fit your personal needs.

Medical Caveat: Whether you are an "endurance athlete" or a "power athlete," you should consider the following. If you have had kidney disease, occasional urinary tract infections, or gouty arthritis, your doctor may encourage you to replace half of your animal proteins with plant proteins, or reduce total protein intake to 10% of calories.

Some endurance athletes, such as distance runners or distance swimmers, find it helpful to adjust their ratio to 65/20/15: 65% from carbs, 20% from fats, and 15% from protein (females); Males might adjust it to 60/20/20. You should never drop the fat intake below 20% of daily calories.

Some power athletes, such as football and softball players, find it helpful to adjust their ratio to 55/25/20: 55% from carbs, 25% from fats, and 20% from protein. Unless you are insulin resistant or over age 40, there is hardly a good reason to increase protein intake to more than 20% of daily calories.

It is helpful to know your cholesterol levels and triglycerides, TAGs (fats). To check these, ask your athletic trainer or doctor where to get a blood test, called a "lipid panel." It will list your "good" and "bad" cholesterols and triglycerides (fats floating around in your blood). Once you have the results, you can examine two ratios: total chol. to TAGs and total chol. to HDL. If your total cholesterol number is more than 2 times the triglycerides, and your HDL (good) cholesterol is 40 or lower, you are probably eating too many fast acting (high glycemic) carbohydrates (page 120) for your activity level. So, if this is the case, try decreasing your % of carbohydrate by 5% to 10%. And eat more vegetables!

You should also figure your ratio of total cholesterol to HDL. It is one of the best ways to determine your risk of getting heart disease and other degenerative ("wear and tear") diseases like diabetes, as you age. If your total cholesterol is only 3.5 times larger than your HDL, you have a very low-risk ratio. Please see the chart below.

3.5	very low risk
3.5 to 4.5	low risk
4.5 to 5.5	moderate risk
5.5 and higher	high risk

If you checked 4 or more items on the insulin resistance questionnaire on page 31, you may have inherited a tendency toward insulin resistance and diabetes. A common problem, insulin resistance means the cells in your body resist the job of insulin, which is to shuttle nutrients into your cells. When the gates to your cells are closed, glucose and insulin levels stay high in the blood, and fat-storage is switched on. You should consider reducing your percentage of carbohydrates to 50% of daily calories, and mostly from lower glycemic food sources, such as fresh vegetables and whole grains. (Please see table of Glycemic Indexes of Popular Sports Foods, page 120) Also, consider raising your protein to 25% to make up the lost calories. Eating protein with every meal tends to control fat storage

Write your personal goal for daily nutrient distribution. **Example:** 60/25/15. (You might refer to the chart on page 15.)

Daily Nutritional Goal		
carbohydrates		%
fats		%
proteins		%

STEP 3
Eat the Right Meals
at the Right Times

STEP 3:
Eat the Right Meals at the Right Times.

Now, you can calculate how many grams of each nutrient you need each day. For example, if your TDEE is 3,000 calories, and your nutrient distribution is 60/25/15, you would multiply .60 by 3,000 calories, which equals 1,800 C—the number of calories you should get from carbohydrates throughout the day. Next, since 1 gram of carbohydrate equals 4 calories, you would divide 1,800 by 4 to get the number of grams of carbohydrate per day.

Example: 1800/4 = 450 grams of carbohydrate you need per day.

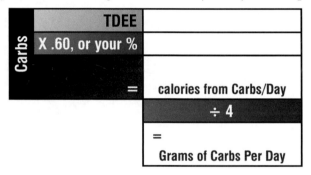

You can now do the same calculations for fats and proteins. But when you figure the fats, be sure to divide the calories by 9, because 1 gram of fat = 9 calories. Protein, however, gives you the same number of calories per gram as carbohydrate does: 4.

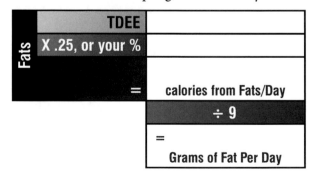

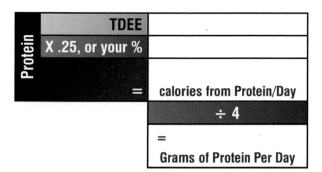

	TDEE	
Protein	X .25, or your %	
	=	**calories from Protein/Day**
		÷ 4
	=	
		Grams of Protein Per Day

Please write your daily need for carbs, fats, and proteins in grams below.

Carbohydrates	Grams/Day
Fats	Grams/Day
Proteins	Grams/Day

Example of Daily Nutritional Breakdown in Grams

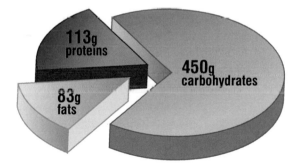

If an athlete needs 3,000 calories per day, and their nutrient ratio is 60/25/15, then he or she should consume roughly 450 grams of carbs, 83 grams of fats, and 113 grams of proteins per day to maintain the current muscle mass and body weight.

To gain weight, shoot for a safe rate of one pound per week. Large athletes may gain more than one pound per week when they start training after a layoff. This means you need to increase your daily intake by 500 calories if you are untrained or haven't worked out in several weeks. If you are well trained, you may need to increase your daily calories by 700 to 1,000. So, for the athlete who needs 3,000 C per day, he or she should consume between 3,500 and 4,000 C/day to gain one pound of muscle per week. These extra calories should come from the same balanced ratio of foods, not all from protein or all from carbohydrates. If you follow the instructions in the rest of this handbook, your gains should be from muscle, not fat.

If your goal is to lose fat, shoot for a safe rate of 1 to 2 lbs per week. (1 lb if you are a relatively small person, 2 lbs if you are big.) This means you need to decrease your daily intake or increase daily activity by 500 to 1,000 C/day, or use 25% of your TDEE. Working out twice a day while decreasing your daily caloric intake by 25% usually works. If you follow the instructions in the rest of this handbook, your weight loss should come mostly from loss of fat, not muscle.

If your goal is to gain muscle and lose fat at the same time, focus on gaining muscle, and take more daily walks than normal. Be sure to get six meals a day. The increased muscle mass will raise your metabolic rate and help to burn fat.

You may have heard that virtually every athlete should eat about six meals per day. A great deal of research supports this. *(Benardot, Verboeket, Jenkins, Burke, Phillips, Williams)* Eating more often helps to suppress fat gain and to maintain muscle tissue throughout the day. It stabilizes blood sugar, which is very helpful for athletes who are somewhat insulin resistant. Stable blood sugar promotes steady energy levels throughout the day, instead of experiencing highs and lows. Six smaller meals satisfies hunger so you don't gorge yourself at dinner. Simply divide the grams you need of the three nutrients by 6 to get the number of grams of each nutrient you need per meal. Your six meals should be fairly similar in size, not three large meals and three small snacks.

The athlete with the 3,000 calorie-per-day diet should find a way to get about 75 g of carbohydrates per meal (450g per day divided by 6 meals = 75g), 14g of fats (83g/6 = 14), and 19g protein (113g/6 = 19g) per meal. When you know this about your meals, it's easier to choose foods and portion sizes. So, one athlete's goal

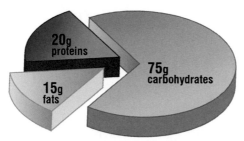

Example Nutritional Breakdown Per Meal

for nutrient ratio per meal may be roughly 75g/15g/20g. This means that the carbohydrates of one meal should weigh about four times more than the proteins, and the fats should weigh three fourths as much as the proteins (keep in mind that most protein sources contain fats too. If you don't have the food labels to read, you can learn to estimate. Please memorize your per meal ratio of nutrient grams from page 37. Now turn to page 107, Appendix B, and write it on your daily tracker in the space provided.

When possible, read the nutrition facts label on most packages. It will tell you the number of grams of each nutrient per serving. Be sure to read the serving size. If you can't read the nutrition label, then you need a few "rules of thumb." 75 grams of carbohydrate is 3 to 5 servings. For example, two slices of bread provide about 30 grams of carbohydrate, one cup of milk provides about 12 g, and a fist-size serving of rice or potatoes is 30 to 40 g.

The following items contain approximately 30 grams of protein: one chicken breast; a piece of lean meat the size of a deck of cards plus one cup of milk; one cup of cottage cheese added to a large apple; a double cheeseburger, or 4 oz of fish, meat or poultry.

Fats are a bit more difficult to eye-ball. It's best to read the nutrition labels on the bottles or packages. For example, one tablespoon of olive oil contains 14g of fat, which for some athletes is enough fat for one meal. A half-inch thick slice of butter is about 12g of fat. Keep in mind that olive oil is more healthful than margarine or butter. Remember to multiply the grams of fat by 9 to get the number of calories. Ex: 12g butter X 9 cal = 108 calories.

Six meals are the key! Start with breakfast, let's say at 7:30 a.m. Skipping breakfast causes a loss of lean body mass, fat to form after lunch, and overeating in the evenings to make up for missed calories. Set a goal never to skip breakfast! If you have to put a yogurt and granola bar in your backpack or briefcase to eat on the way to school or work, so be it.

Two and a half hours after breakfast, you reach for a peanut butter or turkey sandwich, carrots, yogurt and water bottle, and enjoy your second meal "on the run" if you have to. At around 12:30, you eat lunch. Less than three hours later, you eat an energy bar that contains the right ratio of nutrients for meal four. During and after your workout, you drink your recovery drink, which adds to the energy or protein bar to make one meal.

Two and a half hours later, you eat dinner. Finally, one to two hours before bed, you raid the fridge and cupboards for your sixth meal of the day. The meals approximately follow your personal distribution of nutrient percentages. Be sure to consume protein every time you eat. It helps to maintain muscle and stabilize blood sugar and insulin levels.

Eating well doesn't have to be expensive. Check the grocery ads from the newspaper (usually on Sundays), and buy what's on sale at a reduced price. **The "gotta havits" for most athletes are the following: peanut butter, whole wheat bread, oatmeal, frozen vegetables (steam them or heat with a little water in the pot), apples, oranges, bananas, frozen chicken breasts, yogurt, beans, turkey lunch meat, tuna fish, carrot sticks, olive oil, eggs, cottage cheese, soy milk, and whole grain cereal.** If you keep those foods in your cupboard and refrigerator, you are set.

Some people don't like tomatoes, but they want the powerful nutrition that tomatoes provide. One tasty way to do that is to buy a can of "Stewed Tomatoes, Mexican Style," then chop it up into salsa. Add a clove of garlic and one jalapeno pepper, if you wish. It's a quick and easy way to make delicious, homemade (sort of) salsa! Some people eat this salsa with just about anything, especially on scrambled eggs.

To get a printout of a sports menu customized to your individual needs, the following website is highly recommended:
TriSystemNutrition.com/trisystemsportsnutritionbook.htm

SUPERFOODS

A book by Steven G. Pratt, M.D. and Kathy Matthews, *Superfoods: Fourteen Foods that will Change Your Life,* lists fourteen powerful foods that are not only super nutritious, but also help to prevent diseases:

Beans, blueberries, broccoli, oats, oranges, pumpkin, wild salmon, soy, spinach, green tea, tomatoes, turkey, walnuts, yogurt. *(Pratt, 2004. HarperCollins Publishing, Inc. NY, NY)*

You'd be smart to eat as many of these as possible at least once a week.

FOOD PYRAMIDS

I don't mean to start a war here, but I prefer the Harvard Healthy Eating Pyramid over the US Government's pyramid, and I'll tell you why. Professors and nutritionists at the Harvard School of Public Health created the HHEP based on mountains of research over the past 15 years. I believe that the USDA Food Guide Pyramid, recently reborn as the MyPyramid, shows the tense relationship between science and the powerful food

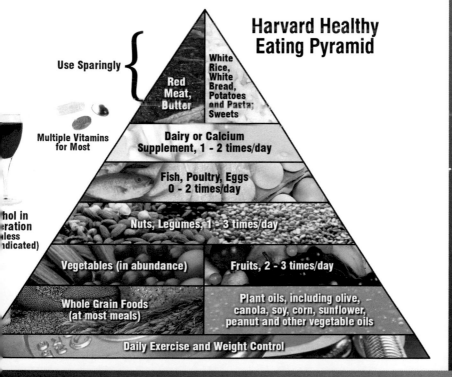

Harvard Healthy Eating Pyramid

Use Sparingly { Red Meat, Butter | White Rice, White Bread, Potatoes and Pasta; Sweets

Multiple Vitamins for Most | Dairy or Calcium Supplement, 1 - 2 times/day

Fish, Poultry, Eggs 0 - 2 times/day

hol in ·ration ·less ·dicated) | Nuts, Legumes, 1 - 3 times/day

Vegetables (in abundance) | Fruits, 2 - 3 times/day

Whole Grain Foods (at most meals) | Plant oils, including olive, canola, soy, corn, sunflower, peanut and other vegetable oils

Daily Exercise and Weight Control

industry. It suggests that half our grains should come from refined starch. Not good, because refined starches act like sugar by adding empty calories, play roller coaster with our metabolism, and increase the risks of diabetes and heart disease. The MyPyramid also lumps red meat together with poultry, fish, and beans; however, these protein sources contain different types of fats, and red meat should be separated from the other more healthful protein sources.

The Harvard Healthy Eating Pyramid sits on a foundation of daily exercise, which is crucial to long-term health. Next, the food choices are described from most important to least important: whole grains, plant oils, vegetables, fruits, fish, poultry, eggs, nuts, legumes (beans), dairy or calcium supplements, red meat, butter, white rice, white bread, potatoes, pasta, sweets, multiple vitamins, and alcohol. Theoretically, if a person consumes a lot of whole grains, plant oils, vegetables, fruits, and good-fat proteins, they will not need vitamins; however, a multi-vitamin containing small amounts (less than the RDA) of vitamins and minerals is recommended as "insurance" even by the conservative JAMA, the *Journal of the American Medical Association*. (June 2002)

NUTRIENTS 101

For those of you unfamiliar with nutrients, here's a brief explanation. There are six major nutrients (eight, if you count fiber and alcohol): water, carbohydrates, fats, protein, vitamins, and minerals.

Water is the most important nutrient because we can't live very long without it. It supports the entire physiology of the human body, and muscles are 70% water. Get used to carrying and sipping a water bottle all day. Drink it continually so that your **urine stays pale yellow, almost clear.**

Carbohydrates are molecules of carbon and water. They are also called sugars or saccharides. Some are chemically small—simple, and some are big chains of sugars—complex. Sugars come from grains like wheat and oats, fruits, vegetables, dairy products, nuts and beans. They provide blood sugar, raise insulin in the blood, and store energy in the form of liver and muscle glycogen. They also can be converted to fat when you eat too much of them.

Sucrose, glucose, glucose polymers, and dextrose get into the blood fastest. That's why sports drinks contain them. Fructose is not ideal for sports drinks because it must go to the liver to be broken down, and that takes time, and fructose can upset the stomach during exercise. Fruit and vegetable sugars enter the blood moderately fast, depending on how much fiber is eaten with the fruit and whether the fruit or vegetable is mostly glucose or fructose. For example, a ripe banana has more glucose than a greenish-yellow unripened banana contains; therefore the riper banana will raise blood sugar faster. During exercise, slamming down 100 to 200 grams of carbohydrate all at once can start reverse osmosis in the intestines, pulling water from blood circulation to the colon and causing diarrhea. *(Bonci, Leslie)* Diarrhea during competition is not fun! Most athletes can handle only about 20 grams of carbohydrate every 10 to 15 minutes of exercise.

Sugars from whole grains and fibrous vegetables, not overcooked, generally get into the blood the slowest, so they keep blood sugar up for longer periods. Cooked vegetables, such as potatoes and carrots, put a great deal of glucose into the blood, which causes the pancreas to raise insulin in the blood, turning on fat storage. So, eat a sizeable source of protein, such as 20% of the meal's calories, and some fat with cooked carrots or potatoes; the protein and fat moderate the absorption of glucose and calm the insulin response.

Distance athletes should consume 1 to 1.5 grams of carbohydrate per kg of body weight per hour of exercise. *(Clark, N., Tobin J., Ellis, C.)*

Dr. Dan Benardot teaches that during exercise, a 200-lb athlete can normally tolerate up to 60 grams of carbohydrate per hour. A 100-lb athlete should consume half that much. *(Bernadot)* **As a general rule, an athlete's daily consumption of carbohydrate would be 4 grams of carbohydrate per pound of body weight.**

For example, a 150-pound athlete would consume 600 grams of carbohydrate per day. Over six meals, that's 100g per meal: for example, 1 fruit, 1 potato and a sandwich for one meal.

Fats are necessary to make hormones, cell membranes, and to protect the body from injury and extreme temperatures. Chemically, fats are carbon skeletons, linked by either single or double bonds to hydrogen. Single bonds are stronger than double bonds. Saturated fats are full of single chemical bonds of hydrogen, so they don't break down well in the body and can cause problems. Polyunsaturated fats (liquid vegetable oils) have two or more double bonds, so they can react chemically in the body. Monounsaturated fats, prominent in olive and avocado oils, have one double bond and are also better for you than saturated fats. *(Benardot)* Mono and polyunsaturated fats are healthful, because they don't tend to cause disease

of the heart, plaque in blood vessels, and fatty liver as much as saturated fats do. But we need some saturated fats too.

Solid, white fat, such as shortening, becomes trans fat when heated to liquid. Trans-fats tend to cause heart disease. You should minimize the amount of solid fats—margarine, butter, shortening—that you eat to 20% of your total fats. Better for you are the liquid fats like olive oil, sunflower oil, peanut oil, canola oil and other vegetable, nut and plant oils.

Essential Fatty Acids (EFAs) are not made in the body. You have to eat them. Omega 3 fatty acids are very healthful at about 1000 mg per day. You get it from cold water fish and plant foods like black currant seed and flax seed. Omega 6 is also in fish and vegetables, but you need much less of it.

Proteins are made of amino acids. Your body can make 11 of the 20 amino acids, but you have to eat the other nine. When all 20 amino acids are available, your body can make antibodies to fight germs, hormones to operate your systems, bones, cartilage, muscle, skin, hair, and nails. Obviously, you need enough of these critical amino acids. The animal proteins have the most complete set of amino acids. Fish, chicken, turkey, eggs, soy and dairy products

150lb man X .8g = 120g protein/day

are good sources. Sources of incomplete proteins are whole grains, beans and some vegetables. Mixing beans with whole grains can give you all the essential amino acids.

Can a vegetarian be a healthy athlete? Yes, if they get enough of the nine essential amino acids by eating a variety of vegetables, soy products and whole grains like rice and wheat. Beans and long-grain rice combine to make a complete protein. Some veg etarians will eat eggs and/or dairy products; however, vegans eat no animal products. They usually need to supplement the diet with Vitamin B12 because B12 is well absorbed only from animal products. Vegetarian athletes may need to take an iron supplement because exercise requires an increased demand of oxygen carrying capacity from hemoglobin and myoglobin, both of which are built with iron, and the best dietary source of iron is red meat.

How much protein do I need? The debate wages on! Some books tell weight lifters to eat at least one gram of protein per pound of body weight per day. Other books say one gram is twice as much as you need. I agree with the most respected sports scientists. The ACSM, American College of Sports Medicine, is a very highly respected source of information on athletic performance. Its official position states that endurance athletes need 1.2 to 1.4 grams **per kilogram** of body weight per day, and power athletes need 1.6 to 1.7 grams per kilogram of body of weight. In grams **per pound** of body weight, that amounts to roughly .6g and .8g respectively; therefore, recommending just under one gram per pound of body weight is wise. Excess protein is associated with urinary calcium losses. Since calcium is necessary for bone strength and normal muscle contraction, you don't want to be at risk for weak bones or muscle cramps.

Peter Lemon, a world famous authority on protein metabolism, recommends .7 to .9 grams per pound of body weight per day for athletes. Indeed, just less than one gram per pound is the respected recommendation. *(Lemon)*

The ACSM differs slightly from some of the top sports scientists in its recommendation for endurance athletes. Some claim that endurance athletes need as much protein as power athletes because they burn up a significant amount of muscle protein (branched-chain amino acids) during prolonged exercise. My recommendation is **.7g for endurance athletes and .8g per pound of body weight per day for power athletes.** Excess protein is stored as fat, turned into glucose for energy, and excreted through the kidneys. The increased urinary output removes water and minerals like calcium, which promotes dehydration and over time can cause kidney disease. If you insist that consuming more than one gram of protein per pound of body weight has put more muscle on you, it's likely because of the increased calories the extra protein provided. You can get the extra muscle-building calories more healthfully from carbohydrates.

Training improves the body's ability to use protein, so there is no need to increase protein intake as training progresses. Lifting weights breaks down muscle protein, but over the next 48 hours muscle protein is rebuilt to result in a net gain. *(Tipton, Wolfe)* Having a lot of muscle glycogen helps to prevent the breakdown of muscle proteins. *(Lemon)*

Animal proteins can lower the ph of the blood, making the blood more acidic than plant proteins do. Acidic blood tends to promote fatigue, infections, arthritis, and an environment for other diseases. It is a good idea to eat more plant protein and less animal protein. Try drinking soy milk instead of cow's milk, eat a soy burger instead of a beef burger, or eat more beans and rice instead of pork chops. And eat more vegetables to help balance the ph of your blood.

STEP 4
Recover Fast, Heal Quickly, and Prevent Illness

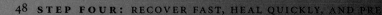

STEP 4:
Recover Fast, Heal Quickly, and Prevent Illness

RECOVER FAST

You have a 30-to 45-minute nutritional "window of opportunity" after exercise to do three all-important things: speed up the reconstruction of glycogen in muscles, decrease the damaging effects of the hormone cortisol, and start protein synthesis for maximal muscle building. Use a drink with a ratio of 3:1 or 4:1, fast acting carbohydrates to whey protein, with 1 gram of glutamine and leucine, and 250 mg Vitamin C and 200 IU of Vitamin E. Vitamins C and E are antioxidants which fight the free radical scavengers that damage tissue and cause disease. One to two extra grams of glutamine per day can lower the risk of illness, such as respiratory infections, from strenuous exercise.

You can purchase a carb/protein drink, or make one yourself for less money. I mix two quarts of a sports beverage with 30 grams of plain or vanilla whey protein, shake it up, and drink one cup about 15 minutes before my workout. During exercise, I'll drink another three cups (along with more plain water if I'm sweating heavily), then drink the second quart after the workout, within 30 minutes. When two hours have passed since the end of the workout, I eat a real food meal that has more protein than carbohydrate. That keeps blood sugar levels strong without spiking them, which facilitates protein synthesis. This routine is backed by both American and international clinical studies. *(Ivy, Portman)*

Would you shake hands with fifty people in the morning before they have showered? You can imagine what disgusting body fluids and germs you would pick up! That's what happens when you work out at a gym, grabbing weights and machines. If you're not wearing gloves or washing your hands thoroughly right after the workout, don't be surprised if you get a gnarly infection.

Wash your hands often, and sleep about nine hours per night to strengthen your immune system and to maximize muscle growth. Keep a **regular routine** as much as you can. On the night before a big event, sleep your normal hours. If you are used to eight hours of sleep, stay with eight, not ten or eleven. On game day, eat foods you are accustomed to.

HEAL QUICKLY FROM BRUISES AND OTHER INJURIES

Thankfully, many schools have athletic trainers to help with post-exercise soreness and injuries. But you too should know a few things. The dog may be man's best friend, but ice is definitely the athlete's best friend. Use the RICE acronym: Rest, Ice, Compression, Elevation. Rest the injured part, Ice it, Compress it with a wrap, and Elevate it above the heart when possible. Apply ice for one to three days to new bruises, sprains, and strains. Fill a plastic bag with small ice chunks; it should be quite heavy. (Grocery store produce bags work well.) Put the **ice bag** right on the skin, no towel between, for 15 to 20 minutes. **The burning and aching for a few minutes is normal, then it gets numb.** Do that several times for a couple of days.

If it's a minor injury that allows movement with little or no pain, then keep it moving the next day. Movement pumps blood in and out of the injured area. Blood flow brings in nutrients and takes out waste products. If the injury is severe, you may be forced to keep it immobilized for a while. See your athletic trainer or a doctor.

Eat a balanced diet of fruits, vegetables, whole grains and lean proteins. Use a couple of supplements, such as vitamin C, proteolytic enzymes, and MSM to shorten healing time.

PREVENT ILLNESS

Dehydration is out of alphabetical order on this page, because it is the number one cause of poor athletic performance, and I want to stress it. Working muscles can produce 20 times more heat than when at rest. To get rid of the heat, the body sweats. When you are not fully hydrated, you have less blood circulating, so your heart has to pump faster to get oxygen and critical nutrients to your cells for energy and growth. The more dehydrated you get, the faster your heart has to work, which generates more heat, and the less your body can cool itself from the extreme heat of exercising. It takes only a 2.7% loss of fluids to hinder athletic performance. *(Barr, Magel)*

When you work out, you would be foolish not to have water or preferably a sports drink available, with about 15 grams of carbohydrate for every 8-ounce serving of liquid. Drink 4 to 8 ounces (1 cup) every 15 minutes (general rule), depending on the humidity and your sweat rate. A distance athlete should drink at least one quart or liter per hour, more if in high humidity and/or if he or she is a large athlete. If you have difficulty tracking how many cups or liters you are drinking, use a "rule of thumb" that says one average gulp/swallow is approximately equal to one ounce, so **eight swallows are roughly one cup of fluid.**

When you train in a humid environment, your body can't cool itself nearly as well as in a dry climate. The body cools itself by putting sweat from heated blood on the skin's surface so the air can dry it off by evaporation. (Skin wetting can help reduce sweat loss and keep you more hydrated.) The blood beneath the skin's surface is cooled, then returns to the heart and cools the inner body. But if the air is already holding a lot of water—humidity—it doesn't pull the sweat off your skin very fast. So the body has to sweat more and more, and you get drenched in sweat, but are not cooling well. Soon, you get dehydrated from losing so much water, and you are unable to sweat much at all. If your body can't sweat, your core temperature rises to dangerous levels, causing heat stroke, brain damage, and sometimes death.

Athletes with a great deal of body fat are at greater risk of heat stroke because the fat insulates the body, keeping heat in and cold out. Sometimes even an ice bath won't stop the heavy athlete from "cooking" to death. Athletes with 30% or higher body fat should not work out until their urine is pale yellow to "clear-ish." They should drink at least a cup of sports drink every 10 to 15 minutes, more if in a hot, humid environment. The sodium in sports drinks helps to keep water in the blood circulating compartment, so you can sweat, and sodium drives the urge to drink. It is not uncommon for large football players to lose up to 12 lbs in one day after two-a-day workouts.

A good way to figure how much fluid you need to replace is by weighing yourself nude before practice. Then using a bottle of sports drink, keep track of how much you drink during the workout. After practice, weigh yourself again dry and nude. If you are two pounds lighter, you have lost 32 ounces (4 cups) of sweat. If you drank 16 ounces (1 lb) during practice, then you would have lost 3 lbs if you hadn't drunk anything. So, you now know you need to drink 32 ounces more, for a total of 48 ounces, during the workout to maintain the hydration level you had before practice. You could get two more 16-ounce bottles and use them at practice, or keep refilling one bottle.

Adonis Complex describes a distorted body image some muscular people have. Though very muscular, they see themselves as too thin. This can lead to drug abuse and other unhealthful practices.

Arthritis, though rare among young athletes, can be painful and hurt athletic performance. There are many types, and they normally bother older people. Unless your doctor diagnoses an auto-immune disorder (like rheumatoid arthritis), it's likely to be osteoarthritis, the wear and tear of joints from doing something the same way over and over again with force or gravity acting on the joint. In heavy people, regular running or walking will sometimes cause osteoarthritis in the knees. Weight lifters who repeat the same lifts the same way for years are also prone to osteoarthritis.

Asthma is a narrowing of air tubes in the lungs, caused by exercise or allergic reactions to dust, foods, pollen, pets or dirty air. Athletes can often help the situation by getting more Omega 3 oils (fish and flaxseed) and less Omega 6 oils (vegetable oils). Also, eating more tomatoes or tomato products, pink grapefruit, watermelon and beans can reduce the symptoms of asthma. *(Applegate)*

Female Triad Syndrome is a vicious cycle of not having normal menstrual periods, losing calcium from bones (which leads to osteoporosis), and starting heart disease. It occurs when a female athlete is lacking calories, exercising too much, or both—which are often caused by an eating disorder. See page 130 for characteristics of anorexia nervosa and bulimia. If you are missing periods and are trying to lose weight, you need to talk to a counselor right away!

Gouty Arthritis occurs when uric acid levels get too high in the blood, then start to make crystals in joints of low blood circulation, such as the big toe. It's a problem with metabolism of protein. Uric acid is not the same as urea, the normal waste product of protein metabolism excreted through the kidneys in urine. Genetics is commonly to blame for gout. Gout normally rears its ugly head first as a red, sore, big toe. If you are eating lots of protein and notice a sore big toe, and it wasn't smashed, kicked or stepped on, you should see a doctor right away!

Headaches are common among athletes. The usual causes are emotional stress, trauma (bumps on the head), loud music with no ear plugs, lack of sleep, bad posture, caffeine, and too much sugar. So, logically you would work on minimizing those factors. Sleep deprivation is a big problem for college students. It takes self-discipline to get to bed on time, which is difficult for many college freshmen. Set limits on your evening socializing, like no more than two nights a week. Some studies show that taking 400 mg of Riboflavin daily for three months can reduce the number and severity of migraines. *(Applegate)* Because pain relievers (NSAIDS) like aspirin, Tylenol, and ibuprofin can slow muscle recovery and can damage liver and kidneys after prolonged use, an alternative to consider is a good chiropractic adjustment of the upper spine.

Heart Problems among young athletes are rare and typically inherited from parents. Some people have a propensity toward high blood pressure, irregular heartbeat, or atherosclerosis (plaque buildup in blood vessels). If your blood pressure is above 140/90, you should not work out with heavy weights. Stay with lighter weights and work on muscle endurance. If you have noticed unusual flutters or heart palpitations, please see a cardiologist. Sometimes an athlete will get dizzy or faint after working out. It happens if you stop abruptly without a cool down. Blood pools in the exercised muscles, so less is available for the brain to keep you alert. For more information on assessing your cardiac risk, see www.heart.org.

Hyperhydration is the opposite of dehydration. Can you drink too much water? Yes, if you exercise in the heat for 3 to 5 hours, drink only plain water, and haven't eaten salty foods for a few days. Sweating removes electrolytes like sodium from the body, so plain water dilutes the body's electrolytes too much, and you get sick with hyponatremia: low sodium. A marathon runner who doesn't drink sports drinks is at risk for hyponatremia. Symptoms include nausea, fatigue, headache, and collapsing.

Muscle cramps can mess up your game and be very painful. The actual cause is not well understood, but we first look at an electrolyte imbalance. Low sodium, low potassium, and low or high calcium can cause cramping. It occurs when the muscle is fatigued. Eating fruits, vegetables, lean meats, and drinking a good sports beverage can help, along with good, slow stretching during and after workouts.

If nutrition is not the cause, then look to the nervous system. Nerves send electrical charges to muscles that can excite them or shut them down. These nerves are sometimes irritated at the spine or at a joint like the knee. Physical therapy or a good chiropractic adjustment can reduce pressure on nerves and help muscles work better.

Muscle soreness usually begins the day after an intense workout. It is caused by inflammation in the muscle from tiny injuries to the cells. It is not caused by lactic acid. Within about two hours after exercise, lactic acid has been removed from muscles and sent to the liver for detoxification. The best ways to minimize DOMS—delayed onset muscle soreness—is not to overwork the muscle in the first place and to help it recover quickly by feeding it a drink right after the workout that is a 3 or 4 to 1 ratio, carbs to proteins, and lots of water. Then keep moving as much as reasonable over the following 24 hours. Movement helps muscles pump out the waste products through the blood.

Overtraining Syndrome (OTS) is a sad occurrence because it is preventable. Fatigue, nausea, weakness and depression all make the life of student-athletes miserable and may force them to quit. It happens from poor nutrition more than from too much exercise. If an athlete is sleeping well, keeping well-hydrated and eating enough calories from a healthy sports diet—roughly 60% of calories from fruits, vegetables, and whole grains (carbs), 25% from good fats like fish, olive and other plant oils, and 15% from lean proteins like turkey, fish, beans, whole grains, soy, and dairy products—OTS should never happen!

Sports Anemia is closely related to the Female Triad because the usual cause is inadequate nutrition. Iron deficiency is the usual cause of sports anemia. Of all the food sources of iron, red meat provides the most absorbable iron. If an athlete is avoiding red meats, he or she may not get enough iron, which is desperately needed to build red blood cells that carry oxygen to every cell in the body. Female vegetarians are at high risk for iron deficiency anemia, partly because of blood lost from menstruation, and partly because of not getting enough iron from the diet. Another athlete at risk for anemia is the distance runner. The repeated pounding of feet on the ground damages red blood cells which carry iron in the hemoglobin.

STEP 5
Take Effective Supplements

STEP 5
Take Effective Supplements

Advertisers target you. They know that athletes are very motivated to excel and are willing to try almost any supplement to improve performance. Sickness and even death sometimes occur because of misuse of a supplement. Either the supplement hadn't been tested enough, the athlete overdosed on it, or the supplement did not fit the athlete's body and metabolism.

This section includes the findings of scientific research on the use of supplements, including recommendations, which you should not take lightly. To a large degree, your health and success in athletics depends on how carefully you apply the following information on supplementation.

THE REAL SCOOP ON OVER 50 SUPPLEMENTS

SUPPLEMENT GRADES	
A	Use some of these.
B	These may help you.
C	Wait for more studies.
D	Save your money.
F	Avoid these.

A GRADE SUPPLEMENTS

The A grade means there are many well-designed studies about them, they work, and they are safe when used as directed. If you refuse to use any of them, you are not serious about reaching your potential.

Creatine: Countless studies have proved its effectiveness and safety in building muscle mass and strength, when taken in the right amounts. If you are a power athlete who needs explosive strength and quickness, creatine is worth trying. Start for 4 to 5 days of loading the muscles with 20 to 25 grams a day, spreading out the doses over the day. *(Burke)* Then maintain with 2g to 5g per day with 1g glucose per kg of body weight **within one hour after exercise.** Excess creatine is excreted in the urine.

If a power athlete is eating a vegetarian diet, she or he **must** supplement with creatine to achieve optimal performance, because creatine is found in meat. *(Lukaszuk)* Creatine supplementation also improves performance in intermittent, high intensity sports, such as soccer, and it reduces the effect of lactic acid buildup, thereby improving endurance. *(Preen)* It is believed that creatine may help events such as 400- to 800-meter runs. It may also improve mental alertness after exercise. *(Hogervorst)* Creatine supplementation increases muscle cell diameter and the size of the protein parts (micro filaments) of muscle cells. *(Greenhaff, Harris, and Casey)* Taken with caffeine, the benefits of creatine are wiped out.

Glucosamine and Condroitin help to provide the building blocks for cartilage repair. They can reduce the symptoms of osteoarthritis and promote healing after a sports injury, but they may also increase insulin resistance. Some studies have shown it to reduce pain as well as pain-relieving drugs, but without the side effects. Try 500 mg a day for a month for joint pain. *(Burke)*

Iron is essential for the oxygen energy system in transporting oxygen to all the body cells. *(Williams)* Williams found it to be slightly deficient in Americans, especially in women and teenagers. Women who have heavy menstrual periods are at risk for iron deficiency anemia. It is a concern for endurance athletes because running damages red blood cells when the feet repeatedly pound the pavement. Red blood cells carry iron and oxygen. Also, females and athletes who train at high altitudes are at risk. You can get iron from lean red meats, chilibeans, green leafy vegetables, and iron pots and pans. Vitamin C helps it to be absorbed. If you are female and don't eat red meat, you should consider a supplement of 18-40mg a day on a mostly empty stomach. *(Constantini, Beard, Tobin)*

Omega 3 Fatty Acids (EPA, DHA): For overall health, this is a must! The American Heart Association stated that these have heart-protective effects, and they are essential, meaning the body can't make them; you have to eat them. Cold water fish and flaxseed oil are the best food sources. Omega 3 may not be specifically termed as performance enhancing in sports, but it is usually lacking in the typical American diet, so I want to stress its importance. Some studies showed it reduces the inflammation from fatigue and overexertion, that it increases oxygen delivery to muscles, and reduces muscle soreness. A study by Dr. Luke Bucci indicated that Omega 3 fatty acids may improve strength and speed; however, Cheuvront noted that O3 fatty acids, though essential for health, do not by themselves enhance athletic performance. They just tend to keep you alive and well longer!

Plant oils: This is another item that is low in the typical American diet. The Harvard School of Public Health places plant oils next to whole grains at the bottom of its healthy eating pyramid for two reasons: 20% to 30% of our daily calories should come from fats, and plant oils help to protect against heart disease. Because most Americans consume too much margarine and meat fats and don't get enough plant oils, this needs to be stressed as a "supplement." Olive oil, canola oil, soy oil, avocados, peanut oil and other vegetable oils are some of the most healthful plant oils for your body. They are good for the heart and nervous system. Please cook with olive oil when possible, and use it in salad dressings (with or without vinegar). Dr. Ben Markham recommends a mix of olive, coconut, and sesame seed oils to cook with.

Proteolytic Enzymes: bromelain, papain, trypsin, chymotrypsin. Football players at the University of Pittsburgh experienced faster healing times for minor injuries than players on a placebo (fake supplement). The University of Delaware showed that the enzymes shortened injury recovery time from 8.4 days to 3.9 days. *(Burke, E.R.)* Pineapple and Papaya are good food sources of proteolytic enzymes; otherwise, check a health food store. A normal dose is 250mg to 750mg three times a day.

Vitamins and Minerals: Generally speaking, athletes don't need more vitamins and minerals than non-athletes need; however, there is some research that shows the need to pay particular attention to certain vitamins that are toxic in high amounts and two vitamins that tend to get depleted in athletes faster than in non-athletes. For example, too much Niacin blocks the release of free fatty acids from adipose tissue, which could hamper ultra-endurance athletes, and excess B6 can lead to nerve damage. Exercise causes oxidation in the cells, meaning that free radicals emerge and damage other cells, which can lead to disease. Vitamins C and E work together to reduce the scavenging free radicals, which damage tissue and promote cancer and heart disease.

The U.S. Olympic Committee recommends no more than 3-20 mg of beta carotene, 250-1000mg Vitamin C, and 150 to 400 IU of Vitamin E per day. Evans said a small supplement of antioxidants can minimize lipid peroxidation and tissue damage and is insurance against a "not so good" diet or intense physical activity. *(Evans)* The body needs 13 vitamins to run its biochemical reactions.

Vitamins and minerals are very small nutrients that trigger chemical reactions in the body. Everybody needs a little of all of them, but too much of any can cause disease. Fruits contain some of the vitamins and minerals we need; vegetables contain some others; grains contain others; meats, beans and nuts also have some. You can't get what you need if you eat the same few foods all the time. You must consume a variety. Try new foods regularly, but not on game day; you don't want to risk getting an upset stomach.

Unfortunately, some student-athletes experience an occasional day without vegetables; therefore, a multi-vitamin supplement is good insurance. Choose a daily vitamin mineral supplement that has low doses—less than the RDA—of everything. (See pages 124-126 for the RDAs.) It doesn't have to be expensive. To aid in digestion, break the pills in half, because some are as hard as rocks, passing through your gut to the toilet without being absorbed.

Many athletes eat a vitamin enriched cereal once a day, such as Total or Product 19. On those days, you don't need a supplement pill. *(Please refer to Appendices F and G for what you should know about vitamins.)*

B GRADE SUPPLEMENTS

The B grade means there is some good research, they are safe when taken as directed, and they are somewhat effective for most athletes.

BCAAs: Branched Chain Amino Acids taken during prolonged exercise raised BCAA levels in blood and reduced muscle degradation. BCAA supplements raised mental alertness after a soccer match and a 30 km race, also reduced the RPE (rating of perceived exertion). *(Blomstrand)* Mittelman found that BCAA supplements before and during exercise delayed exhaustion by 12%. If adequate carbs are not available, BCAAs can improve performance and cognition after the race. During extended exercise, BCAAs, such as leucine, isoleucine and valine supply up to 15% of the muscle's energy needs. Whey has a strong percentage of BCAAs. One gram of leucine (and one gram of glutamine) should be added to your workout recovery drink. *(Ivy, Portman)*

Caffeine: a stimulant of the brain and spinal cord, it speeds up the heart rate and raises blood pressure. It also makes you urinate more. Caffeine raises mental alertness of endurance athletes *(Hogervorst)*. It increases the force of muscle contraction by stimulating calcium in the sarcoplasmic reticulum, which is a tiny, working part of a muscle. *(Tarnopolsky and Cupido).* Bucci found it raised free fatty acids in blood during exercise in those who did not drink any caffeine for 5 to 7 days prior to their event. Graham noted that caffeine reduces the perceived effort and therefore improves performance. If taken with liquids, there is no net loss of body fluids or dehydration.*(Armstrong, Clark)* If taken in pill form, dehydration is more likely. Caffeine raises B-endorphins during exercise, which elevates mood and lowers perception of pain, delaying fatigue by blocking adenosine receptors.

Caffeine's effect of making exercise seem easier is one of its two proven benefits. The other is the effect of warm coffee on promoting bowel movements to clean you out before exercise, which some athletes like to do. Keep in mind, however, how you feel before competing. If you tend to get "psyched up" already without caffeine, adding caffeine could "freak you out" with jitters and diarrhea. One can of Red Bull, for example, is enough for many athletes who are not accustomed to drinking caffeine. More than two cups of coffee before exercise is not recommended. One pill of 200 mg caffeine is plenty for most athletes, but they have to drink a lot of water to compensate for the extra urination, because there's not much water in caffeine pills.

The International Olympic Committee bans the use of caffeine in a large enough dose to detect 12mcg in urine. About six to eight cups of coffee within 12 hours would be enough to cause a failed urine test.

Glutamine: an amino acid that your body makes from other nutrients. Glutamine is the most abundant amino acid in the blood. It helps deliver excess amino groups from muscles to the liver and kidneys. Studies indicate it boosts immune function and keeps athletes from getting sick as often. *(Kingsbury, Billings, Parry)* Oral glutamine can raise HgH (growth hormone) levels and increase muscle cell volume. It also stimulates glycogen synthesis in the liver during recovery. It can help to prevent OTS (overtraining syndrome) and muscle breakdown from strenuous exercise. Budgett reported that glutamine may enhance immune function to prevent overtraining syndrome at doses of 8g to 20g a day. (This dose includes the glutamine you get from food.) Dr. Newsholme of Oxford University found that low blood levels of glutamine increased the incidence of OTS.

Glycerol, Glycerine, "Glycerate" can help endurance athletes to superhydrate before competition. It holds water, staving off dehydration and delaying fatigue. Drink 36 grams of glycerol in a liter of water for each 100 lbs of body weight two hours before exercise. Then drink another liter 30 minutes before the race. *(Wagner)*

HMB, hydroxy methyl buterate, a byproduct of leucine metabolism, increased muscle mass in untrained athletes at 3g per day. *(Nissen)* Another study showed that HMB reduced the breakdown of muscle tissue during the first 3-5 weeks of training or in prolonged training by endurance athletes. S. Nissen, U of Iowa, found that 1.5g/day increased strength by 13% and 18.4% in subjects who took 3g/day. Iowa State University found that 3-5g/day reduced muscle damage in distance runners and increased leg strength after running.

Melatonin is a popular sleep aid. Darkness triggers the release of natural melatonin from the pineal gland in the back of the brain to help people sleep. Some people don't produce enough, so supplementing with .5 to 3mg in the evening usually helps to induce sleepiness. Ask your doctor before trying melatonin.

MCT Oil is a medium chain triglyceride that has been found to be a quick source of energy, to spare lean body mass, and to help mobilize body fat stores for energy. *(Benardot)*

MSM reduces inflammation and aids in healing joint injuries. Drs. Daniel Sanchez and Mark Grosman treated a large number of sports injuries every day. They found that MSM had very low toxicity, and it shortened healing time. Patients using MSM healed faster and required 40% fewer office visits. *(Burke)*

PS, Phosphatidylserine reduced cortisol during exercise. Thomas Fahey, Ed.D, Cal State Chico recommends 400mg to 800mg orally per day for weight lifters. *(Fahey)*

Phosphate Salts increased aerobic endurance performance at 1g/meal, 4g/day for 5-6 days. Trisodium phosphate caused endurance benefits. *(Robert Cade, University of Florida, Richard Kreider, Ian Stewart)*

Sodium Bicarbonate and Sodium Citrate fight/buffer the lactic acid buildup during high intensity exercise, thereby delaying fatigue and increasing endurance in sprints and long sprints, such as the 400-meter to 800-meter runs. The recommended dose is 300 mg per kg of body weight per day. Divide the dose over several drinks per day, mixed in water. *(McNaughton, Applegate, Matson, Tran)* Too much at one time can upset your stomach.

C GRADE SUPPLEMENTS

The C grade means that some studies show promising results; other studies show no benefits. Further research is needed.

Alpha GPC is a precursor for acetylcholine, a major neurotransmitter. In some early research, it raised growth hormone levels in as little dosage as 150mg to 400mg. *(Burke)*

Aspartates theoretically increase fat burning and spare muscle glycogen. Wesson and others reported that 10g given 24 hours before a race at 75% of VO2 max increased endurance by 15%, and lowered blood levels of ammonia. Maughan and Sadler found no benefit.

Boron is believed to help prevent osteoporosis and raise testosterone level in the blood. Naghii noted it may increase testosterone, and Nielsen found it can help to prevent osteoporosis.

Bovine Colostrum is the first milk from mammary glands. Its immunoglobulins and growth factors help to keep the digestive tract healthy, so it is known to reduce diarrhea in athletes. *(Gastelu, Hatfield)*

Ciwujia is supposed to increase fat burning, oxygen consumption, and reduce buildup of lactic acid; however, Plowman and Cheuvront noted the studies were not valid or reliable.

Chromium can be helpful for glucose intolerant or type 2 diabetics. UL of 200mcg/day. So far, studies show no benefit for athletes. *(Williams)*

Fat Blockers (Chitosan) act like sticky velcro to grab onto grams of fat in your intestines to keep them from entering the blood. One study found that it works on only 3 or 4 grams of fat per meal—not significant for weight loss. It may, however, improve cholesterol. It is expensive and may hinder the absorption of fat soluble vitamins. *(Applegate)*

Lecithin may increase strength, but Staton found it had no effect. *(Staton)*

Magnesium can help athletes to lose body weight. The UL is 350 mg per day. It is useful in untrained athletes who start to work out. It increased muscular power in one study by Lukaski. Brilla and Gunter found it raised oxygen consumption in runners.

SAM-e, S-adenosylmethionine tends to help control inflammation from osteoarthritis, but it's expensive. *(Williams)*

Selenium is supposed to protect cell membranes from oxidative damage during exercise. It does appear to lower the risk of heart disease and cancer. *(Burke, L.)* at a UL (upper limit) of 200mcg/day.

Valerian is a widely known herbal sleep aid. It works quite well after two to four weeks of taking 600 mg two hours before bedtime. *(Burke, E.R.)*

Zinc helps with growth and wound healing in people who are deficient of zinc. *(King, Keen)* It is sometimes low in wrestlers and other "make weight" athletes. *(Krotkiewski)* You need at least 15mg/day, which is easily consumed in food.

ZMA, a combination of zinc, magnesium and vitamin B6 has been found to impact athletic performance and boost testosterone levels naturally. In one study, ZMA raised total and free testosterone levels by more than 30%. More research is needed. *(Burke, E.R.)*

D GRADE SUPPLEMENTS

The D grade means that well-designed studies show no benefits, and we don't know how safe they are.

Choline helps to form acetylcholine, an important neurotransmitter. There is no evidence that it aids to increase strength or reduce body fat. *(Warber, Buchman)*

CLA, conjugated linoleic acid, is theorized to burn body fat. Zambell and Kreider say no.

Co Q10 is theorized to improve endurance and oxygen uptake. Bucci found this benefit, but more studies say there is no benefit. *(Svensson, Braun, Weston)*

Ginseng is supposed to improve action of the heart, oxygen uptake, blood flow and reduce lactic acid accumulation. Dowling found no athletic benefits.

Glandulars are extracts from animal glands like testes. They were thought to raise testosterone levels, but there is no evidence to support this. *(Williams)*

HCA, Hydroxy citrate, is supposed to burn fat. Kriketos found it doesn't work

HGH: Human Growth Hormone. Promotes growth of bodily tissues, especially cartilage. Yarasheski studied the effect of HGH vs. a placebo. In males who weight trained 12 weeks, some tissues grew, but not the strength or size of muscle fibers. Injections are more effective than HGH taken orally.

Inosine, a nucleotide, helps form purines such as adenine. It is suggested that this would produce more adenosine for ATP. No evidence that it works. *(Williams)*

L-Carnitine is supposed to raise fat metabolism and increase endurance. Wacher, Wagenmakers, and Colombani indicated it doesn't work.

Niacin tends to improve cholesterol. Too much niacin blocks the release of fats from fat tissue, which could hamper ultra-endurance athletes. Also, excess niacin causes burning face, neck and hands. It is sometimes prescribed for high cholesterol. *(Pieper, Heath, Bulow)*

NSAIDS: Non-steroidal anti inflammatory drugs (ibuprofen, acetaminophen, aspirin, etc.) reduce pain and fever, but they tend to delay the healing of sore muscles. *(Williams)*

Ornithine: Dr. Luke Bucci reported that Ornithine at a dose of 170mg per kg of body weight raised levels of HgH, the human growth hormone, but it also caused intestinal distress among many subjects. Williams says it has no anabolic effect.

Pyruvate is supposed to reduce body fat. Kalman found it did, but most studies indicated it did not work.

Ribose is supposed to speed up muscle recovery, but it doesn't. *(Ivy, Portman)*

Taurine is supposed to reduce muscle damage and raise antioxidant activity. We need good studies. So far, no benefit. *(Williams)*

Vanadium tends to improve the effects of insulin and glucose tolerance for Type 2 diabetics. Fawcett said it has no effect on lean mass for non-diabetic weight lifters. UL is 1.8 mg a day. Too much can cause stomach distress.

Yohimbine is supposed to increase serum testosterone levels, but there is no evidence that it has an anabolic effect. *(Williams)*

F GRADE SUPPLEMENTS

The F grade means the risks of harm or death outweigh the potential benefits.

AAS, Anabolic Androgenic Steroids: the minor problems include acne and hairloss; the major problems include aggressive attitudes, hostility, depression, structural changes in heart muscle, lowered HDL (good cholesterol), high blood pressure, impaired muscle tendons raising the potential for rupture, liver disease, cancer, shrunken genitals in men, and enlarged genitals in women, suicide, violent crimes. They are not worth it.

DHEA, a precursor to testosterone, only works on the elderly to improve strength. Same with androstenediol. *(Williams)*

Ephedrine helps to burn body fat, but it can kill if the user is prone to heart arhythmias or other cardiovascular problems. (Most people don't know if they are prone to heart problems.) Pure ephedrine is regulated as a drug. The Consumer Union named it the most dangerous of the major sports supplements. *(Haller, Benowitz)* Spend your money on something else, like good food.

Alcohol: Some athletes like to drink a few beers after a workout or event. I do not recommend it, but some of you have made up your mind that you're going to drink alcohol, regardless of what anyone says. My job is to educate you a little so you can make informed, responsible decisions.

In celebration, teammates can easily get carried away and overindulge, often leading to somebody doing something stupid. Be realistic about the possibility of jeopardizing the reputation of your team and school, not to mention your police record. Saying that alcohol has heart healthy effects is a weak excuse because the University of Wisconsin, Madison, conducted a study that found that purple grape juice provides the same heart healthy benefits as alcohol does. Informed athletes also know that one gram of alcohol makes 7 calories, hence the common "beer gut."

Physiologically speaking, remember that alcohol slows your recovery by delaying rehydration and preventing carbohydrate from getting to your muscles to build more glycogen. If you must drink, alternate a beer with a sports drink, so you don't get as dehydrated. Check your urine the next day. If it's not clearish to pale yellow, you are not ready to compete.

Forty years ago, traveling baseball teams survived mainly on steak and beer. This was one factor causing players to get worn out toward the end of a long season, failing to win their division. Alcohol interferes with one job of B-vitamins, which is to make energy, and alcohol increases the chance for dehydration. *(Benardot)*

STEP 6
Build Muscle and Lose Fat

STEP 6:
Build Muscle and Lose Fat

STARTING AN EXERCISE PROGRAM

Anyone starting to work out again needs to be aware of a few important things:

 It's easy to get excited and do too much the first day or two. Avoid this, or you'll get painfully sore and slow your progress.

 You may gain weight the first few weeks. Muscle absorbs water and is heavier than fat. Also, most gain about 1 pound of blood in their body after one week of exercise.

 You should know how fast your heart should beat to get a good training effect. You could use the following formula: (220 - your age) x .7 = your training heart rate. While working out, pause and place two fingers to one side off the front of your throat (Adam's apple), and count how many times the carotid artery pushes against your finger in ten seconds. Then multiply that number by 6. If your training heart rate is 140 beats per minute, and your heart is beating only 120 times, then increase intensity to raise your heart rate.

If your goal is to gain muscle, add 500 to 1,000 extra calories to the TDEE you figured on page 30. If you see no gain after two weeks, see your doctor about the possibility of inadequate absorption of nutrients from your intestines or abnormal hormone levels.

GAINING MUSCLE

Muscles don't read magazines. No matter how much hype you see in magazines or hear from people, your muscles do not react to it. Your muscles respond to real science, not gimmicks or hype. (Magazines contain some good material too.) They do what your nervous system and nutrition tell them to do. If you give your muscles what they need, when they need it, they will respond well, within their genetic limits. For example, some people gain one pound of muscle in a week by eating 600 extra calories per day; others need an extra 1,000 calories a day to pack on a pound of new muscle. No matter how much a skinny marathon runner lifts weights, he will never look like Arnold Schwarzeneggar.

Three things are required to gain muscle:

1. Adequate sleep

2. Extra calories at the right times

3. Resistance training/weight lifting

ADEQUATE SLEEP:

According to sleep studies, the three key words of good sleep are **Quiet, Cool, Dark.** When you have all three, you sleep best. If your apartment/home is noisy at night, hot, and has light shining through windows and doors, you have some problems to solve.

Our society has created a myth that successful people need less sleep than others. For example, Thomas Edison bragged that he slept only four hours each night; however, he also took two long naps during the day! Adequate sleep is a tough task for many college students. (For that matter, it's difficult for busy adults too.) Students who are not exercising every day can be less responsible about sleep than student-athletes have to be. Regular students can stay up late and catch up on missed sleep during afternoons or weekends, but athletes can't afford this pattern. You have to be ready to perform in your workout every day.

Daily workouts can weaken the immune system, and if you're running on less than ideal sleep, you are more likely to get sick. Successful workouts require good sleep the night before, not the weekend before. One study conducted at the University of Utah by Dr. David Tomb, a psychiatrist, found that the hours before midnight are indeed better for sleeping than the hours after midnight. Falling asleep at 10:00 p.m., for example, puts the brain into the deepest, healthiest sleep right away; whereas falling asleep at 12:00 doesn't allow as much of the deep, therapeutic sleep, regardless of how long you sleep in. So, **when** you sleep is almost as important as how long you sleep.

This is where some students give me the "Yeah, right, I'm lucky to get six or seven hours of sleep per night!" (Actually, that isn't very lucky.) Most athletes need about nine hours of sleep per night. (Teens and young adults need more sleep than the typical 50-year-old.) Some do fine on eight hours, but the majority needs nine. And studies show that sleeping on a regular schedule is better than sleeping different hours each night. *(Harvard Medical School) (Burke, E.R.)*

It is normal for young adults to push the limits and try to get by on less sleep than they need. Because they are young and often feel "invincible" they make their mind and body recover quickly for studies, tests, and social life; however, in the long run, they can suffer from sleep deprivation. Besides making people grumpy, sleep deprivation promotes "colds," impairs mental performance, and can start the process of degenerative diseases, such as arthritis, cancer, autoimmune diseases and heart disease.

Overtraining syndrome and chronic fatigue are common results of sleep deprivation. You may think that you are the exception to the rule of eight or nine hours of sleep. Perhaps you are, but keep in mind that you are "getting by" on seven or fewer hours probably because your hormonal glands are healthy and giving you enough "adrenalin" to keep you going. Eventually, this takes a toll on your system. Please try eight hours for three weeks, and see how you feel.

Muscles grow during sleep, because the body hardly uses any muscle protein to keep you alive while you sleep. Three energy sources keep you alive while sleeping: liver glycogen, blood sugar, and fat. The longer you sleep, the more chance you have to gain muscle because the muscles are building protein instead of breaking it down. Research shows that sleep has an enormous impact on athletic performance. *(Burke, E.R.)*

CALORIES AT THE RIGHT TIME: WHY INSULIN IS YOUR BEST "STEROID."

When you eat can accelerate your fitness to new levels or stifle its progress. Just as fuel injectors provide fuel and oxygen at the precise time the pistons need them, nutrient timing can provide what the muscle needs when it needs it. Many trained athletes reach a "plateau" and are unable to build additional size and strength. This can be overcome by the right timing of your meals and supplements. Recent landmark research has discovered that you can maximize gains by fueling your muscles with a certain amount of nutrients at the right times before, during and after workouts.

When you exercise, two major things happen: 1) besides the rise of epinephrine and norepinephrine hormones, the stress hormone **cortisol** rises in the blood, breaks down muscle proteins, and suppresses your immune system; 2) the workout burns muscle glycogen (stored energy), and muscle fibers are traumatized, irritated and become inflamed. Your goals should be to minimize the damaging effects of cortisol and to replenish the lost glycogen quickly so that muscles can start to make proteins as soon as possible to overcome the loss of muscle proteins. (Note: If a urinalysis shows 3-methyl-histidine, you have damaged muscle fibers too much.)

Right after workouts, muscles are extremely sensitive to insulin, your best anabolic hormone, which if stimulated strongly will lower cortisol and drive nutrients into the muscle cells to build protein and new glycogen. Carbohydrates stop the rise of cortisol by raising the level of powerful insulin in your blood, thereby minimizing the damaging effects of cortisol. The rise of insulin stimulates protein synthesis, inhibits muscle breakdown, and promotes transport of amino acids to the muscle cells. *(UT Health Science Center)* Raised insulin during exercise protects muscle protein from the catabolic effects of cortisol. It also increases blood flow to the exercised muscles more that 100%, which speeds up removal of metabolic wastes like lactic acid, and it delivers nutrients like oxygen faster to the muscle cells.

Adding protein to a carbohydrate drink promotes the metabolism of protein and lessens the demand for amino acid release from muscles, plus it improves protein synthesis after exercise. *(UT, Galveston)* The University of Texas found that a carb/protein drink increases endurance 57% over plain water and 24% over Gatorade, because of its ability to spare muscle glycogen. When you drink a 6% carbohydrate drink (14 g of carbs per 8oz serving) during exercise, cortisol decreases by 80%. *(Bishop, Nieman)* Drinking one cup of the protein/carb mixture a few minutes before exercise increases protein synthesis after exercise. *(UT Galveston)*

Strenuous exercise suppresses the immune system, increasing the risk of infection (usually respiratory) by raising cortisol levels, which weakens the activity of immune cells. Bishop and colleagues at Longborough University in England found that carb supplements could reduce biochemical markers of inflammation by 50%. Antioxidant vitamins C and E reduce CPK, an important marker of muscle damage, 24 hours after a marathon. *(Dr. William Evans, U of Arkansas)* Waiting two hours to eat after workout is a bad idea because it cuts the replenished glycogen in half. *(UT Austin)*

The first step in switching from catabolism (breaking down) to anabolism (building up) after a workout is to raise the level of insulin in your blood. You have a 45-minute window of opportunity after your workout to do this effectively. UT Austin found that a carb/protein drink produced a greater insulin response than either one separately. Insulin increases nitric oxide, NO2, in muscles better than 30g of arginine. *(Laakso)* Vanderbilt

University found that a carb/protein supplement increased muscle protein synthesis six times more than carbs alone and lowered 3-methyl-histidine, a sign of muscle fiber damage. Iowa State and US Marine Corps found that carb/protein supplement lowered medical visits by 33%, infections by 28%, and muscle joint problems by 37%. *(Ivy, Portman)*

A 3:1 or 4:1 ratio of carbs to proteins is best, such as a drink with about 50g of high glycemic (fast acting) carbohydrates mixed with 15g of whey protein. In other words, you want to fuel your body with about 4 times as much carbohydrate as protein right after your workout. Whey protein works best. (You could pour 15 grams of whey powder into one quart of sports drink and shake it up, or buy a drink already mixed.) Waiting 1 to 2 hours allows muscles to become insulin resistant, which makes it more difficult to get the necessary nutrients into muscle cells.

After the recovery drink in the 30- to 45-minute window, follow up with a high protein, low carb meal about two hours after exercise. This helps to maintain high insulin levels and drives more amino acids into muscle cells. This meal can be from a variety of protein sources, not just whey. *(Ivy, Portman)*

To gain muscle, add 500 to 1,000 calories to your TDEE, depending on whether you consider yourself an easy-gainer or a hard-gainer. These extra calories should come from the same ratio of nutrients you have chosen, e.g. 60/25/15, not solely from protein or carbohydrate.

RESISTANCE TRAINING

Hopefully, you have a personal trainer, athletic trainer, or strength and conditioning coach to help you with a strength training program. If not, contact the NSCA, the National Strength and Conditioning Association at www.nsca-lift.org.

Keep the SAID principle (explained on page 97) in mind to accomplish your training goals. When you make your muscles do something new, they respond by adapting to the new activity. In the off-season, you should increase the total amount of weight lifted about every third time you lift so your body is forced to get bigger and stronger. You should not lift weights with the same muscle two days in a row. The muscles need two to five days to fully recover, especially the larger muscles. Remember, lifting weight breaks down muscle protein. No matter how you eat, if you work the same muscles on the next day, it's like pruning new growth off a tree daily, never letting the fruit develop.

LOSING FAT

Losing fat requires burning more calories than are consumed over a given period of time. The healthiest way to do that is to exercise daily and eat fewer calories than you are using. For example, if it takes 2,500 calories to support your daily activities and keep you alive, then on 2,000 calories a day, you should lose weight. So, you either exercise more intensely or eat smaller meals, or both. However, the body has an amazing ability to maintain its comfort size. It's called homeostasis. Your body may fight to stay at 18% body fat, and another athlete's body likes to be at 14%. Realizing this should prevent you from extreme measures which can harm you.

Weight loss lowers your daily energy expenditure, so the same amount of food that got you there ends up causing weight gain. When you are smaller, you need to recalculate your total daily energy expenditure based on the new body weight, then establish your daily caloric goal. *(Saltzman and Roberts) (Benardot).*

Eating six meals a day helps to minimize fat storage, especially when protein is included in the meal. High carbohydrate meals with hardly any protein tend to rev up your fat making engine.

People who fidget tend to lose weight faster than those who sit still. Bouncing the knee up and down under a desk burns more calories than holding still. Also, spicy foods tend to raise metabolic rate longer than non-spicy foods do. But if the spicy foods bother your gastrointestinal tract, stay away from them. The raised metabolism is not worth the irritation or heartburn.

Note: Apples help people to manage body fat by curbing appetite with pectin, one of the best types of fiber. The fiber helps to move food through the intestines, slowing the rate of carbohydrate absorption into the bloodstream, which helps to stabilize blood sugar, curb hunger, and minimize fat storage. Eat an apple with balanced meal of proteins and fats.

BODY FAT

You need fat to make important hormones, to protect your organs, and to provide energy. It is impossible to be healthy without some body fat. Female athletes should have between 17% and 28% body fat. When they fall below 17%, they are in danger of interrupting their reproductive cycle, menstruation, and starting bone disease. Male athletes should be between 5% (marathon runners) and 20% (some power athletes). The last I heard, the lowest body fat % in the NFL was owned by a linebacker for the Baltimore Ravens. His was 7%. 10% to 15% is good for most male athletes.

If you are an athlete with 20% body fat and wish to get down to 15%, use the following formula to set your goal weight:

$$\text{Target body weight} = \frac{\text{Lean mass in pounds}}{1.00 - \text{desired body fat \%}}$$

$$\text{Ex: } \frac{120 \text{ lbs Lean mass in lbs}}{1.00 - .15 = .85} \quad \frac{120}{.85} = \begin{array}{l}141 \text{ lbs} \\ \text{target weight}\end{array}$$

NOTE: If your body fat is not measured by the same person, using the same technique, with skin-fold calipers every time, then be aware of some potential inaccuracies. For example, if it's a machine that works on electrical impedance, your body's hydration level will affect the measurement. Be sure to eat and drink the same amounts during the few hours before each measurement day; otherwise, you will have inconsistent readings.

To calculate how much of your body weight is fat and how much is lean mass, do the following: If skin fold calipers show your body fat to be 20%, and your total body weight is 180, then multiply 180 by .20, and you get 36 lbs of fat on your body. The rest is lean, so subtract 36 from 180 to get the lean mass. Or to get the lean mass amount more quickly, you can multiply 180 lbs by .80 because if your % body fat is 20, then the other 80% must be lean.

STEP 7
Learn From True Stories of Other Athletes

STEP 7:

Learn From True Stories of Other Athletes

The following true stories teach valuable lessons. See if you can relate to any of them.

SHE TOOK SO MANY SUPPLEMENTS THAT SHE FORGOT TO EAT

She was young. She was smart. She was strong. She was fast. She was good-looking. She had big company support. She was the envy of the track world. In spite of all of this, she was miserable that she was getting older and bigger, that her breasts and hips were larger, and that she didn't smash any records at her last meet. So, in spite of her history of successes, she did what all too many athletes do to gain control over the biological clock that never stops ticking. She started "dieting." By the time she came through my lab, her times had slipped away with her weight, and she found herself in a downward funnel of eating that kept sucking her lower and lower. The first thing she said when she walked into the lab was, "The day I graduated from high school my metabolism stopped!" She had decided that the best way to gain control over her age-related biological changes was to eat less (big mistake), and to take supplements to obtain the nutrients she needed to stay healthy and strong (another big mistake).

The results were disastrous on many levels, mainly because she had changed much of what had made her successful. She had been an eater. She ate all the time. She ate before her morning run, after her morning run, at midmorning, at noon, at midafternoon, before her late-afternoon run, after her late-afternoon run, in the early evening, and in the late evening. She learned from the very beginning that this was the very best way to get the *energy* and *nutrients* she needed to meet the needs of her explosive power and magnificent endurance. But she had forgotten what worked for her and decided that eating less was better, and, besides, her health wouldn't suffer because she was taking "supplements."

When I asked her what supplements she was taking, she brought in a gym bag full of everything from B-complex to amino acid powders. When I explained that most of these supplements were useless without sufficient energy intake, she asked what *supplement* she should take to get the energy she needed for the supplements to work on! And then a stunned look appeared on her face, as if she had just awakened to what she had been doing to herself. It was like the sudden realization that smokers sometimes get when they're puffing on a cigarette and complaining of making it up the stairs. It's just one of those moments when the reality of the situation hits you. From that moment on, it was easy to get this world-class runner to do the right thing and start eating again, and she's happier and more successful as a result.

Benardot, D. Chapter 1 story: *Nutrition for Serious Athletes,* Human Kinetics: Champaign, IL ©2000

LEAN AS CAN BE BUT ALL YOU SEE IS FAT

Imagine a talented athlete at the peak of her competitive life. This was an Olympian who was just a hair's width behind the best person on the swim team, and someone who was willing to do anything to make that place hers. Of course, everyone has an inherited physique, and this powerhouse clearly had inherited all the qualities (both good and not-so-good) of her genetic donors. She was on the short side of small and had a block house figure.

Nevertheless, while swimming her laps, there was no one better to look at: great strokes, perfect flip turns, powerful starts off the blocks, a rocket finish—and it all came together to make her one of the best. However, despite her national and international competitive successes, she still wasn't considered the best this country had to offer, and this ate away at her psyche like nothing else could. When I say that she tried everything in her arsenal to get better, I mean just that. She spend more hours practicing, she became more careful about what she ate; and she began bugging her coach for more ideas on how to improve every part of the stroke, even if the resultant improvement would be incrementally miniscule.

Ultimately, she became so unhappy with herself (mind you, this is one of the top swimmers in the world) that she found fault with her appearance. "If only I were leaner…" and "If only I had less fat…" were common interjections in her conversations. It was as if everything ultimately boiled down to a simple equation that said, "less fat equals improved speed." But when you have someone who, for her sport, is already in the 10th percentile for body fat percent, it's hard to imagine that having less fat would cause a competitive improvement. (In fact, swimmers may find that the reduction in buoyancy associated with too little fat can actually increase drag and reduce speed.) Nevertheless, she began seeing herself as fat and took the only dramatic action she could think of—dieting to the point of starvation—to make herself seem less fat. An eating disorder, regardless of how it rears its ugly head, is never an attractive proposition. For an athlete trying desperately to do anything to gain a fraction of a second, an eating disorder can be disastrous.

As part of our regular evaluations, we noticed that all the swimmers in the lab were comfortably walking around in their swimsuits or in gym shorts and T-shirts—all of them except the swimmer in question. She had on two sweatshirts, gym pants, and a jacket and was still shivering. We knew right away we had a problem on our hands, but we also knew we had to document what was going on. As we suspected, she had lost weight and was, therefore, "smaller." However, she had lost more weight from her lean body mass (muscle) than from her fat mass, so she was less able to move her body weight than before (strength-to-weight ratio is critically important in all sports). In fact, she lost in muscle the equivalent muscle weight represented on an entire arm. When we spoke to her coach to see if he had any concerns, he immediately blurted out that she had become impossible to work with. Her starts were short, her turns had deteriorated, and she no longer had a killer finish. All the strength and skills that were at the core of her successes had virtually disappeared. Her coach was ready to increase her training schedule (even though she was already spending more hours in the pool and weight room than anyone else) because he couldn't see how she could compete in the next big competition given her state of unreadiness. Of course, there was no way she could continue to do even what she was now doing, so increasing her training schedule would have been impossible.

When we reviewed her diet, it became clear that she was trying to cover up her eating disorder. It would have been impossible for her to have eaten what she reported she ate (barring a clinical malabsorption disorder) and have lost so much weight. When I became convinced that we really had a serious problem on our hands, I took the only action I knew to take. I convinced her coach to remove her from the team until she presented him with a letter, from a psychiatrist trained to work with eating disorders, clearly stating that her continued participation in competitive swimming would not place her at risk for an eating disorder. In other words, if she wanted to come back, she had to change what she was doing, and she had to convince an appropriate medical professional that this change would not be altered if she returned to swimming. This strategy was not easy to initiate, and it was devastating for the athlete. Imagine trying all your life to be on a team, succeeding in getting on that team, and then being taken off the team because you were trying anything (albeit wrongly) to be more competitive.

Fortunately, this story has a happy ending. She did it. She went home, went to counseling, learned what she needed to do, accepted her physique as it was, ate better, trained smarter, got her OK letter from her physician, and became a star. If you've watched swimming competitions, you've seen her swim and succeed.

Benardot, D. Chapter 3 story: *Nutrition for Serious Athletes,* Human Kinetics: Champaign, IL ©2000

PROTEIN FOR BREAKFAST, LUNCH, AND DINNER

One of my favorite graduate students of all time was a young man who took up competitive bodybuilding after he completed his undergraduate biology degree and several years before he entered our graduate program in sports nutrition. When I first saw him, I knew I didn't want to make him angry, but I came to find out that his muscular appearance did not reflect his

personality. He had the arms the size of my neck, and his legs were the size of my waist, but he was gentle, caring, and very, very bright. When I asked him why he wanted a graduate degree in sports nutrition, he knew exactly why. He was tired of getting information on how to train and how to eat from people who were unqualified, and he wanted to be the purveyor of good information rather than the recipient of bad information.

He took all his core requirements (nutritional biochemistry, nutrition and metabolism, research design, etc.) and finally became eligible to take my class in advanced sports nutrition. During his entire time in graduate school, he was training and competing as a bodybuilder, but he occasionally shared that his successes were not what they should have been. I noticed in class that he was almost always tired and that he was always eating something. He did this discreetly enough, so it didn't disturb anyone. Besides, I'm such an advocate of snacking behavior that I was actually pleased to see an athlete find ways to take in enough energy.

We came to a point in class when we were discussing the various nutritional protocols that might work for different sports, and I asked our bodybuilder if he wouldn't mind sharing what he did to build muscle and stay competitive in the sport. He said he found that the critical thing was to "eat protein all the time, and eat lots of it." Even though this was the standard for so many athletes in the sport (albeit a bad one), I was stunned by his answer. How could someone so educated go down this protein path? His statement, of course, initiated a discussion on whether this was an appropriate strategy and what was happening, metabolically speaking, with all that protein. What came out in the discussion boiled down to this: he knew that eating too much protein could cause difficulties with hydration (getting rid of all that extra metabolic waste from protein causes an increased water loss) and that it wasn't the best fuel for his muscles, but whenever he tried eating carbohydrates instead of protein he started losing weight-and that wasn't something this bodybuilder could afford to do. As it turns out, what he was eating all the time was steak, roasts, and chicken (fried and otherwise), which also has a good deal of fat associated with it. All of this protein *and* fat (fat is a highly concentrated form of energy) helped him maintain his caloric requirement and weight, but wasn't the best combination for muscle function. However, when he tried eating more carbohydrate and less protein, his total energy intake dropped because he was eating almost no fat. I made it a class project to find a way that he could eat the right foods *and* take in enough total energy to maintain (and even build) his muscle mass. The result was lots of fluids with a balanced diet heavy on carbohydrates (about 60 percent of calories), moderate in protein (about 15 percent of calories), and moderately low in fat (about 25 percent of calories), consumed six times per day.

About one year after he graduated, he came back to say hello, and he showed me one enormous trophy with his name on it. He said his change of food intake gave him so much more "energy" that he was able to train harder and longer, and he felt better all the time. Imagine that. Following the science really does work.

Benardot, D. Chapter 5 story: *Nutrition for Serious Athletes,* Human Kinetics: Champaign, IL ©2000

TIMING IS EVERYTHING

There was a talented gymnast at a National Team training camp who could do the skills well enough to make it onto the National Team three years in a row, but she just couldn't break into the top level to compete at the key competitions. She was eager to talk with me when she heard I was the new nutritionist for the team, and she found her way to see me during the first possible rotation. I wasn't ready for what she said as she introduced herself to me: "I'm tired of being calling bubble butt, but I can't do anything about it-and believe me, I've tried *everything!*" It was true that she was genetically predisposed to carrying a bit more fat around the hips than other places, but it was also clear to me that 99.9 percent of all women on the planet would like to look as fit and as athletic as she did. However, in the world of gymnastics, she clearly was carrying more fat than most.

We talked at length about what she had done in the past to lower her body fat, and she told me about past discussions she had had with exercise physiologists and nutritionists-each one putting her on a different exercise regiment and evaluating her dietary adequacy over and over again. It was at this point that she said

something very interesting to me. She explained that at her last visit to the nutritionist, she was told that her total daily caloric intake was almost a perfect match for her daily caloric expenditure. That was even more frustrating for her, since she imagined that having a perfect diet should lead to a perfect physique. I wondered, was her diet really perfect?

I started asking her some questions about her daily schedule and when she ate her meals, and it became almost immediately clear that the calories were right, but they weren't right at the right time. She was "backloading" her food intake because her daily schedule was so busy. This is something that *many* athletes do because they all have incredibly busy schedules. Instead of spreading out their calories throughout the day, they eat a little bit during the day and eat a huge amount in the evening (i.e., backload) to take in the energy they need. (Backloading food intake is a bit like getting into your car in the morning and noticing that the gas tank is completely empty, then saying to the car, "Well, take me to my meeting now, and I'll fill you up once we get there." It just doesn't work that way.) We talked about whether it would be possible to spread out the food and drink throughout the day to avoid hunger and thirst, and to make certain there was enough of the right fuel (i.e., carbohydrate) in the system to train productively. We worked out a strategy for moving a bagel from here to there, and consuming more sports beverage during practice but having less at night, and she agreed to give it a try. (After all, she had tried *everything* else!)

When someone calls you on the phone, you can usually tell if they have a smile on their face while they're talking. Well, she called me about a month after the training camp with a big smile on her face and said she'd never felt stronger and her jeans had never fit better. I was happy for her and said we could talk again at an upcoming competition in two weeks. When we met again, it was as if I was looking at a different person. She was smiling, feeling good, and wasn't carrying around the "bubble-butt" label on her forehead. I took her weight and was surprised that she was about five pounds heavier, and I couldn't have been more happy. For the first time in a long while, her muscles were responding to her hard training because there was enough fuel around at the time the fuel was needed. So, she looked smaller, weighed more, had less fat, and was performing better. She was eating the same food in the same amounts, but eating them when she needed them the most. Timing is everything.

Benardot, D. Chapter 7 story: *Nutrition for Serious Athletes,* Human Kinetics: Champaign, IL ©2000

HOCKEY NIGHT IN ATLANTA

Several years ago, Atlanta had a professional hockey team, a farm team for Tampa Bay, called the Atlanta Knights. I'm not sure if it's possible to have more fun working with a group of athletes than I had working with this group. Besides having the first professional female player, Ms. Manon Rheaume (her presence added a whole new dimension to hockey!), they also had an experienced coach who had done and seen everything in hockey, from the pros to the Olympic Games. When the coach asked me to work with the team to make certain they were doing the right things nutritionally, he invited me to join the team in practice and go to the games to get a sense of what was going on. I also had all the team members in the lab to assess bone density, body composition, and nutrient intake. I learned from my data collection and observations was that these athletes worked hard day after day. When they weren't playing, they were either practicing or traveling somewhere to play. When they were on the ice, it was no-holds-barred all-out skating that was almost as exhausting to watch as it was to do. I also learned that when practice was over or when a game was finished, they didn't have any food in the locker room, so it was often more than two hours after this strenuous activity before they got something to eat. It was this point that I decided would be my first point of attack.

I spoke with the coach about getting some food into the locker room for the players to eat right after practice or a game. My main point was that the high-intensity activity of hockey was depleting their muscle energy stores (glycogen) and that a key to assuring its replacement for the next day of activity was to have 200 to 400 calories of carbohydrate *immediately* following practice. The coach agreed that it was a good idea, so he gave me a small budget, and I put one of my graduate students to work on getting some good-tasting carbohydrates in the locker room. To make it easier, the Gatorade Company donated some Gatorpro (high-carbohydrate meal replacement) and Gatorload (high-carbohydrate supplement) for the team. I explained the importance of having something to eat immediately after practice or the game. I said they should try to eat some food *before* they showered and dressed. After I spoke, the coach said it was a good strategy to follow, and that was that. For the rest of the year, the team ate and drank immediately after practice and games, and they also managed to win the league trophy at the end of the year.

A couple years after the team moved to another city, I ran into one of the players at a restaurant. He told me he had been recruited to play for one of the major league teams and, at the end of his first week there, noticed he was beginning to feel run down. He remembered what I did with the Knights and requested that his new team also have food in the locker room for right after practice and games. He told me the whole team is now eating pasta and French bread in the locker room.
There's just no stopping a good idea!

Benardot, D. Chapter 9 story: *Nutrition for Serious Athletes,* Human Kinetics: Champaign, IL ©2000

TRADITION DOESN'T ALWAYS WIN

Several years ago, the university I worked at hired a top-notch, experienced coach for our basketball team. He did wonders in recruitment, and his practices were, from what I heard, character-building experiences. The team went well beyond its expectations during the first year, chalking up the best season in the history of the university. All this was accomplished despite a team that was, essentially, inherited from earlier recruitment efforts. At the beginning of the next season, disaster loomed ahead. Several of the players were ineligible because of academic difficulties, a couple of recruits were transfers who couldn't play right away because of NCAA rules, and the star guard broke his foot during the first game of the season. The bench was—thin— very thin.

There is no easy game in NCAA Division I basketball, and I've yet to see a game between Division I teams where one team has truly coasted. It doesn't matter if it's a preseason game, an out-of-division game, or a "Holiday Classic," these teams play to win. From a physiological standpoint, it's difficult to imagine anyone who could stand the rigors of an entire game played at the pace these athletes play. Basketball is a sport that combines power and endurance, and it's all-out, be-faster-than-your-opponent-or-you-lose game. When a bench is thin, it forces those who do play into a position where they need all the nutritional training help they can get.

When I observed one of the games, I noticed that the players weren't following an optimal hydration strategy during the game. This was happening despite the good efforts of the athletic training staff, which was obviously trying to do everything within their means to get the players to drink on schedule. Besides, these trainers were busy trying to keep the players they had physically functional

(I've never seen so much tape). After observing this, I thought I'd send off a memo to the coach and athletic training staff to remind them of the importance of what they already knew, that game-time hydration (with carbohydrate) is critical to performance—salting the memo with science as my crutch. The most important response to this memo was that the coach wanted to talk with me. (This, by the way, is a characteristic of all successful coaches. They want all the information they can get, and they want it *now*.) After numerous attempts at schedule juggling, we talked and it all boiled down to this: the university had a contract with a beverage company to supply the sports beverage, and the athletes didn't like it. As a result, the athletes were provided with plain water during the games. Plain water during games has problems, not the least of which is that it doesn't provide the all-important carbohydrate. In addition, because it contains no sodium, it doesn't drive the desire to drink. Therefore, athletes tend to drink less than they need.

After some experimentation, we found a beverage the athletes liked and it was "hidden" in the containers of the contract company. (This is known as win-win solution!) The result was, to say the least, *very* good. The experience helped to solidify my belief that if you have parties willing to listen to the facts, good things will happen.

Benardot, D. Chapter 11 story: *Nutrition for Serious Athletes*, Human Kinetics: Champaign, IL ©2000

STEP 8
Travel Smart

STEP 8:
Travel Smart

Most North American athletes don't travel outside the U.S. and Canada to compete, so they generally don't have to worry about the cleanliness of water or what and where they are going to eat. Sometimes, however, athletes travel to countries where the water contains germs their stomachs can't handle. These can cause severe illness, headaches, diarrhea, cramps, etc. They should ask about the need for bottled water and take some of their favorite foods with them. A sudden change in diet may upset you, so having your favorite energy bars, a fruit and perhaps a can of tuna in the suitcase is a good idea. Ultimately, athletes usually find that the food is very good in other countries.

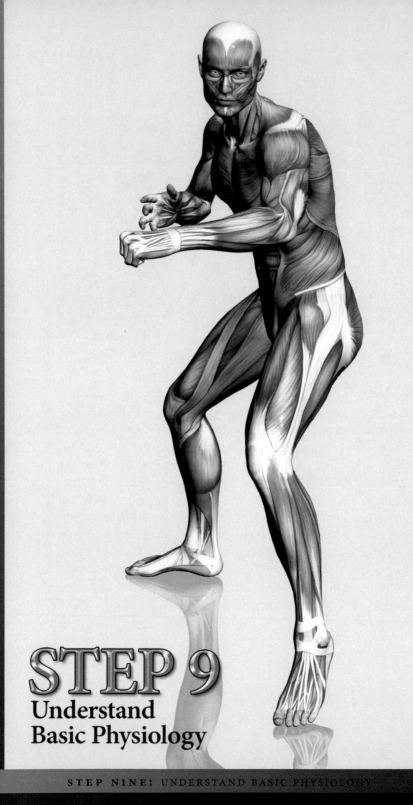

STEP 9
Understand
Basic Physiology

STEP 9:
Understand Basic Physiology

MUSCLE FIBER TYPES

Every muscle in your body has fast-twitch cells and slow-twitch cells; some of the fast-twitch fibers can change to be either faster or slower. The slow-twitch muscle fibers (Type I) contain more oxygen, mitochondria (energy producing parts), and blood, so they are often termed "red". These red cells are slow and can work for a long time—like the tortoise—before fatigue. The fast-twitch fibers (Type II) are called "white", are more explosive, powerful and fatigue sooner—like the hare. Some muscles have more slow-twitch than fast, and other muscles have more fast than slow.

Endurance athletes, like marathoners and distance swimmers, tend to have more slow-twitch fibers than fast fibers in their legs and arms. Sprinters' muscles, on the other hand, contain more fast-twitch fibers. **Some of the fast-twitch fibers can change with training to become more slow-twitch by gaining more mitochondria and blood vessels;** therefore, power athletes can gain more endurance through aerobic/cardio training, but they may lose some power and quickness. Because of this, sprinters and competitive weight lifters should not do much aerobic training during the season of competition. Two or three weeks of aerobic/cardio training before the season should be enough to achieve some cardiovascular fitness, then they can maintain it during the season with short, intense cardio sessions.

This is one reason why many power athletes struggle to manage their weight after their playing days. Their muscles have been trained to be fast-twitch with low blood supply and few mitochondria. These muscle fibers burn fat very poorly because fat burns in the presence of oxygen. So, the athletes tend to gain fat easily.

ENERGY SYSTEMS

The body uses nutrients in four ways to make energy. The first way is through phosphocreatine (PhCr) that is sitting in the

Fates of Blood Glucose

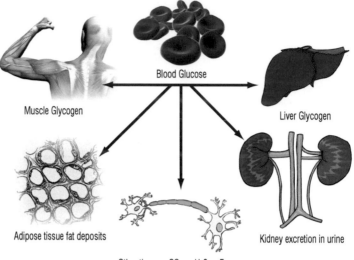

Muscle Glycogen

Blood Glucose

Liver Glycogen

Adipose tissue fat deposits

Kidney excretion in urine

Other tissues: CO_2 + H_2O + Energy

After assimilation into the blood, glucose may be stored in the liver or muscles as glycogen or be utilized as a source of energy by these and other tissues, particularly the nervous system. Excess glucose may be partially excreted by the kidneys, but major excesses are converted to fat and stored in the adipose tissues.

muscle cells. When you sprint all out, you can use the PhCr system for about eight seconds. Second, blood sugar and glycogen (stored carbohydrate) in the muscles kick in to give you energy. Athletes can go pretty hard for about 1.5 minutes on glycogen. Third, the oxygen systems take over because you have to slow down to breathe in more oxygen. In the presence of oxygen in the muscle cells, fats and amino acids (proteins) are burned for fuel, along with a continued use of muscle glycogen. Fourth, your body pulls more glucose (blood sugar) into muscle cells from the blood to make energy.

Drinking a sports beverage that contains carbohydrate and protein during exercise drives glucose into the blood within minutes. This can spare some muscle glycogen. Basically, the longer you exercise, the more fat and muscle protein you burn. Keeping glucose and amino acid levels strong in the blood during exercise can minimize the breakdown of muscle proteins and glycogen.

Burning fat gives you a lot of endurance, but when glycogen and blood sugar are used up, you fatigue. The best way to keep energy and strength throughout competition is to train your body to store a lot of glycogen in the muscles and to drink fluids continually. You do this by working out intensely and consuming plenty of carbohydrates, especially the week before competition. Be sure to read the section on carbo-loading on page 99.

THE S.A.I.D. PRINCIPLE: SPECIFIC ADAPTATION TO IMPOSED DEMANDS

The structures of your body adapt to the demands imposed upon them. Your muscles and bones get bigger and stronger after you make them lift more weight than they are used to lifting if you feed them right. Your heart and skeletal muscles gain more endurance through distance training. Another way to think of the SAID principle is by saying, "Practice makes perfect." To get good at soccer, you have to play soccer. For your body to adapt to swimming, you have to swim.

When you are in training, your body is trying to get faster, stronger and more skilled based on the workout demands you impose on it. It can't adapt without the right tools: the nutrients. It needs water, carbohydrates, fats, proteins, fiber, vitamins and minerals. **The best way to get these nutrients is from real food.** Real food has phytochemicals you normally don't get from pills or shakes. Real food is satisfying, and real food helps to prevent diarrhea and constipation.

Providing the right nutrients to support the SAID principle requires planning. You have to think ahead about what and when you are going to eat. Six meals a day work best, but it is difficult at first glance to do this. If it were easy, every one would be fit, and your competition would be tougher. One of the best uses of your handbook is to help you plan and track your six meals each day. You should look at your weekly schedule for each semester (pages 80 through 90), write in your classes, and decide when you can eat your six meals. Try to space them about every 2½ to 3 hours.

STEP 10
Be Ready on Game Day

STEP 10:
Be Ready on Game Day

CARBOHYDRATE LOADING

Carbohydrate loading is one of the best inventions since sliced bread! It increases muscle endurance in activities lasting 90 minutes or more. The more glycogen you have stored in your muscles, the longer it takes you to fatigue. So it makes sense to enter a competition with your muscles packed full of glycogen. You do that by gradually tapering down the intensity and amount of exercise for five to seven days prior to the event until you are doing very little or no exercise on the day before. Maintain your diet at about 65% carbohydrate during the seven days of reduced exercise. By eating more carbs than you are burning for a few days, the muscles collect large amounts of glycogen, and you are ready to roll on game day. Sometimes the muscles get full and stiff, which may hamper flexibility. Carb loading does not enhance short sprints or power sports like baseball and gymnastics. *(Sherman/Costill Method, Benardot)*

For athletes who forgot to carbo-load the week before their event, or who can't stand to miss a day of sweating, you can sprint to exhaustion on the day before your event, then carbo-load for as little as 24 hours. This, too, works pretty well. *(Clark)*

PRE-GAME MEALS

What and when to eat before competition has long been a hot topic. Here are five things the pre-game meal should do for you:

- **It should allow enough time for your stomach to be mostly empty when you compete.**
- **It should not cause gastrointestinal distress.**
- **It should satisfy hunger.**
- **It should put plenty of glucose (blood sugar) in your blood and muscles.**
- **It should increase body water.** *(Williams)*

The best time for a pre-game meal is three to four hours before competition. If that is not possible, two hours will be fine if the meal is not large. *(Clark)* You can eat 2 grams of carbohydrate per pound of body weight four hours before competition. If you need to eat one hour before a workout, .5 grams of carbohydrate per pound of body weight is recommended before moderate exercise. *(ACSM et al. 2000, Clark p. 99)*

The pre-game meal should be lower in fat than your typical meal. Eat foods you are familiar with, ones that don't upset your stomach. Focus the meal on whole grains, fruits and vegetables, with small amounts of protein. Two grams of carbohydrate per pound of body weight is a general rule. It's a good idea to avoid spicy foods if you tend to get "heartburn." Other foods to avoid before competition are beans, bran, high sugar, and large amounts of protein. Between the meal and your event, sip on a sports drink until your urine is clear to pale yellow.

Appendices

The following pages are for you to use as you see fit. You may photocopy the Tracker pages for your personal use, or order a package by calling the publisher.

On the Daily Tracker sheets, you may wish to write weekly or daily goals. Examples of goals are the following: "Eat at least three servings of vegetables every day"; "Eat a balanced breakfast every day this week"; "Get to bed by 10:30 Monday thru Thursday nights." At the end of the week, you can use a 1 to 10 scale to rate how well you met your goals for the week. As the weeks pass, see if your average score climbs a little each week. Make notes on why you think you achieved a goal or why you didn't.

In the nutrition section of the Daily Trackers, you might write what you ate before a workout, then how you felt during and after exercise. You might jot down the foods you rely on to get six meals a day. You may write the amount of grams of nutrients contained in the food servings you typically eat. You may even make a grocery shopping list.

Appendix A:

SPORTS AND NUTRITION TRIVIA

1. Which spreads contain the least heart-damaging fat?

A. Butter
B. Tub margarines
C. Stick margarine

2. What is the literal meaning of the word "gymnasium?"

A. School for naked exercise
B. Sweat Room
C. Sport class

3. Match the following animals to their top running speed.

Human	32mph
Lion	25mph
Giraffe	45mph
Elephant	35mph
Kangaroo	27.9mph

4. Nutritionists recommend eating at least three servings of vegetables and two fruits per day. How many Americans do this?

A. 1 in 4
B. 1 in 7
C. 1 in 11
D. 1 in 20

5. Fact or Fiction? If you stop exercising, your muscle will turn to fat.

A. Fact
B. Fiction

6. Fact or Fiction? Eating fiber helps to control your weight.

A. Fact
B. Fiction

7. The Badwater Ultramarathon stretches 135 miles and is typically run in what temperature?

A. 115 F
B. 90 F
C. Boiling point
D. 45 F

8. Who introduced the freestyle swim stroke to Europe by beating the famous Brits' breaststroke in 1844?

A. Australians
B. Chinese
C. Native Americans
D. Brazilians

9. Fact or Fiction? Pedaling backward on an elliptical trainer works your butt and hamstrings better than pedaling forward.

A. Fact
B. Fiction

10. Which is the best source of calcium?

A. One cup of spinach
B. One cup of plain yogurt
C. One cup of cottage cheese

11. Besides not using their hands, what is the biggest difference between ancient Mayan basketball and modern-day basketball?

A. Wooden ball
B. Losers were sacrificed
C. Nobody cheered

12. 90 minutes of intense exercise depresses the immune system. What's the best way to prevent this?

A. Work out in low altitude
B. Drink 30g of carbs per half hour
C. Take Vitamin C

13. Why would people of Crete Circa who eat a lot of fat experience low rates of heart disease?

A. Exercise
B. Genetics
C. They eat fish and olive oil

14. The following foods have been proven to contain what kind of properties? Garlic, soybeans, cabbage, ginger, licorice root, carrots, celery and parsley

A. Stolen Properties
B. Anti-depressant properties
C. Cancer-protective properties

Answers:

1. B 2. A 3. Human: 27.9mph, Lion: 32mph, Giraffe: 35mph, Elephant: 25mph, Kangaroo: 45mph 4. D 5. B 6. A 7. A 8. C 9. B 10. B 11. B 12. B 13. C 14. C

Appendix B:

SUNDAY
Daily Exercise Tracker

Rating (1-10)

Exercise Goals

Cardio Exercise	Time/Distance/Intensity	Notes

Strength Training	Wt.	Sets	Reps	Notes

Exercise Review

may be photocopied for personal use

SUNDAY
Daily Nutrition Tracker

Rating (1-10)

Nutrition Goals

Meal One	Notes

Meal Two	Notes

Meal Three	Notes

Meal Four	Notes

Meal Five	Notes

Meal Six	Notes

Nutrition Review	Nutrient Ratio
	Carbs:
	Fats:
	Protein:

may be photocopied for personal use

MONDAY
Daily Exercise Tracker

Rating (1-10)

Exercise Goals

Cardio Exercise	Time/Distance/Intensity	Notes

Strength Training	Wt.	Sets	Reps	Notes

Exercise Review

may be photocopied for personal use

MONDAY
Daily Nutrition Tracker

Rating (1-10)

Nutrition Goals

Meal One	Notes

Meal Two	Notes

Meal Three	Notes

Meal Four	Notes

Meal Five	Notes

Meal Six	Notes

Nutrition Review	Nutrient Ratio
	Carbs:
	Fats:
	Protein:

may be photocopied for personal use

TUESDAY

Daily Exercise Tracker

Rating (1-10)

Exercise Goals

Cardio Exercise	Time/Distance/Intensity	Notes

Strength Training	Wt.	Sets	Reps	Notes

Exercise Review

may be photocopied for personal use

TUESDAY
Daily Nutrition Tracker

Rating (1-10)

Nutrition Goals

Meal One	Notes

Meal Two	Notes

Meal Three	Notes

Meal Four	Notes

Meal Five	Notes

Meal Six	Notes

Nutrition Review	Nutrient Ratio
	Carbs:
	Fats:
	Protein:

may be photocopied for personal use

WEDNESDAY

Daily Exercise Tracker

Rating (1-10)

Exercise Goals

Cardio Exercise	Time/Distance/Intensity	Notes

Strength Training	Wt.	Sets	Reps	Notes

Exercise Review

may be photocopied for personal use

WEDNESDAY
Daily Nutrition Tracker

Rating (1-10)

Nutrition Goals

Meal One	Notes

Meal Two	Notes

Meal Three	Notes

Meal Four	Notes

Meal Five	Notes

Meal Six	Notes

Nutrition Review	Nutrient Ratio
	Carbs:
	Fats:
	Protein:

may be photocopied for personal use

THURSDAY
Daily Exercise Tracker

Rating (1-10)

Exercise Goals

Cardio Exercise	Time/Distance/Intensity	Notes

Strength Training	Wt.	Sets	Reps	Notes

Exercise Review

may be photocopied for personal use

THURSDAY
Daily Nutrition Tracker

Rating (1-10)

Nutrition Goals

Meal One	Notes

Meal Two	Notes

Meal Three	Notes

Meal Four	Notes

Meal Five	Notes

Meal Six	Notes

Nutrition Review	Nutrient Ratio
	Carbs:
	Fats:
	Protein:

may be photocopied for personal use

FRIDAY
Daily Exercise Tracker

Rating (1-10)

Exercise Goals

Cardio Exercise	Time/Distance/Intensity	Notes

Strength Training	Wt.	Sets	Reps	Notes

Exercise Review

may be photocopied for personal use

FRIDAY
Daily Nutrition Tracker

Rating (1-10)

Nutrition Goals

Meal One	Notes

Meal Two	Notes

Meal Three	Notes

Meal Four	Notes

Meal Five	Notes

Meal Six	Notes

Nutrition Review	Nutrient Ratio	
	Carbs:	
	Fats:	
	Protein:	

may be photocopied for personal use

SATURDAY
Daily Exercise Tracker

Rating (1-10)

Exercise Goals

Cardio Exercise	Time/Distance/Intensity	Notes

Strength Training	Wt.	Sets	Reps	Notes

Exercise Review

may be photocopied for personal use

SATURDAY
Daily Nutrition Tracker

Rating (1-10)

Nutrition Goals

Meal One	Notes

Meal Two	Notes

Meal Three	Notes

Meal Four	Notes

Meal Five	Notes

Meal Six	Notes

Nutrition Review	Nutrient Ratio
	Carbs:
	Fats:
	Protein:

may be photocopied for personal use

Weekly Review

Rating (1-10)

Weekly Exercise Tracker

Top Moment of the Week

Cardio Exercise Notes

Total Sessions	Total Distance	Total Hours

Strength Training Notes

Total Sessions	

Ratings on How Well Goals Were Met

may be photocopied for personal use

Weekly Review
Weekly Nutrition Tracker

Rating (1-10)

Favorite Meals of the Week

Nutrition Review	Nutrient Ratio
	Carbs:
	Fats:
	Protein:

Ratings on How Well Goals Were Met

Meal Planning for Next Week

Meals	Grocery List

may be photocopied for personal use

Appendix C:

GLYCEMIC INDEX
OF POPULAR SPORTS FOODS

Food	GI	Food	GI
High GI (>70)		Powerbar, chocolate	56-83
Glucose	100	Potato, boiled	566
Corn Flakes	92	Rice, white long grain	56
Honey, Canadian	87	Rice, brown	55
Potato, Baked	85	Boost, vanilla	53
Potato, microwaved	82	Kidney beans, canned	52
Gatorate	78-89	Orange juice	52
Rice cakes	78	Banana, overripe	52
Jelly beans	78	Pumpernickel bread	50
Cheerios	74	Ensure, vanilla	48-75
Cream of Wheat, instant	74	Peas, green	48
Graham crackers	74	Lentil soup	44
MET-Rx Bar, vanilla	74	Spaghetti, no sauce	44
Bread, white Wonder	73	Candy bar, milk chocolate	43
Bagel, Lender's white	72	Chickpeas, canned	42
Watermelon	72	Apple juice	40
Bread, whole wheat	71 (52-87)	Strawberries	40
Grape-Nuts	71	**Low GI (<40)**	
White rice	71	PR-Bar, Ironman chocolate	39
Moderate GI (40 - 70)		Apple	38
Sugar, white (sucrose)	68	Pear	38
Cranberry Juice	68	All-bran cereal	38
Snickers	68	Ice cream	36
Stoned-wheat thins	67	Chocolate milk	34
Cream of Wheat, regular	66	Fruit yogurt, low-fat	33
Oatmeal	66	M&Ms, Peanut	33
Mars Bar	65	Milk, skim	32
Couscous	65	Apricots, dried	31
Powerade	65	Banana, underripe	30
Raisins	64	Lentils, boiled	30
Coca-Cola	63	Peach	28
Cytomax	62	Milk, whole	27
Raisin Bran	61	Barley	25
Muffin, bran	60	Grapefruit	25
Corn	60	Fructose (fruit sugar)	24
Grapes	60	Peanuts	13
Sweet Potato	59		
Met-RX vanilla	58		

Data from food companies, K. Foster-Powell, S. Holt and J. Brand Miller, 2002, "International table of glycemic index and glycemic load values," *Am J Clin Nutr*, 76: 5-56; and Gretebeck R. et al., "Glycemic index of popular sports drinks and energy food," *J Am Diet Assoc*, 2002, 102 (3): 415-416

Additional information about the glycemic index can be found at www.mendosa.com/gilists.htm

Appendix D:

CARBOHYDRATES IN COMMON FOODS

To fuel your muscles, the foundation of every meal should be carbohydrate-rich foods. To determine your carbohydrate needs precisely, you can target 3 to 5 grams of carbohydrates per pound (7 to 11 grams per kilogram) of body weigth (ACSM 2000)

For example, if you weigh 160 pounds (73 kilograms), this comes to 480 to 800 grams, or about 60 percent of a 3,200- to 5,300-calorie diet—a range of fuel appropriate for an active person of that weight. Note that this method of calculating carbohydrate needs works best for active athletes with high calorie needs, not for sedentary people.

Food labels are the handiest source of carbohydrate information. The following list of carbohydrate-rich foods can help you keep a tally.

Food	Amount	Carbs (g)	Total Calories
Fruits			
Raisins	1/3 cup	40	150
Banana	1 medium	25	105
Apricots, dried	10 halves	20	85
Apple	1 medium	20	80
Orange	1 medium	15	65
Vegetables			
Spaghetti sauce, Prego	1/2 cup	22	120
Corn, canned	1/2 cup	15	70
Winter squash	1/2 cup	15	60
Peas	1/2 cup	10	60
Carrot	1 medium	10	40
Green Beans	1/2 cup	5	20
Broccoli	1/2 cup	5	20
Zucchini	1/2 cup	2	10
Bread-type foods			
Hoagie roll	1	75	400
Bagel, Thomas's	1	57	300
Pita	1 average (3 oz)	46	240
Tortilla	1 large (2.5 oz)	36	220
English muffin	1	25	120
Bread, rye	1 slice	15	80
Waffle, Eggo	1	14	90
Saltines	5	10	60
Graham crackers	2 squares	10	70

Food	Amount	Carbs (g)	Total Calories
Breakfast cereals			
Grape-Nuts	1/2 cup	47	210
Raisin Bran, Kellogg's	1 cup	45	190
Granola, low-fat	2/3 cup	45	210
Oatmeal, maple instant	1 packet	30	160
Cream of Wheat, cooked	1 cup	25	120
Beverages			
Apricot nectar	8 oz	35	140
Cranraspberry juice	8 oz	35	140
Apple juice	8 oz	30	120
Orange juice	8 oz	25	105
Cola	12 oz	39	155
Milk, chocolate	8 oz	25	180
Gatorade	8 oz	14	50
Beer	12 oz	13	145
Milk, 2%	8 oz	12	120
Grains, pasta, starches			
Baked potato	1 large	50	220
Baked beans	1 cup	50	260
Rice, cooked	1 cup	45	200
Lentils, cooked	1 cup	40	230
Stuffing, bread	1 cup	40	340
Spaghetti, cooked	1 cup	40	200
Ramen noodles	1/2 package	25	180
Entrees, convenience foods			
Macaroni and cheese, Kraft	1 cup	48	410
Bean burrito, frozen	5 oz	45	370
Spaghettios	1 cup	37	180
Lentil soup, Progresso	12 oz	33	210
Refried beans, canned	1 cup	32	200
Sweets, snacks, desserts			
Fruit yogurt	1 cup	50	225
Frozen yogurt	1 cup	44	240
Pop-Tart, blueberry	1	36	200
Fig Newton	1	11	55
Oreo	1	8	50
Honey	1 tbsp	15	60
Maple syrup	1 tbsp	13	50
Strawberry jam	1 tbsp	13	50
Cranberry sauce	1 tbsp	7	30

Nutrient data from food labels and J. Pennington, 1998, *Bowes & Church's Food Values of Portions Commonly Used*, 17th ed. (Philadelphia: Lippincott).

Appendix E:

COMPARING PROTEIN CONTENT

Animal proteins	Protein (grams)
Beef roast, 4 oz cooked*	30
Chicken breast, 4 oz cooked	35
Tuna, 1 can (6.5 oz)	30-40
Egg, 1	6
Egg White, 1	3
Plant proteins	
Soy milk, 1 cup	7
Lentils 1/2 cup	7
Baked beans, 1/2 cup	7
Peanut butter, 2 tbsp	9
Tofu, 1/4 cake (4 oz)	11
Dairy products	
Milk, yogurt, 1 cup	8
Milk powder, 1/3 cup	8
Cheese, cheddar, 1 oz	7
Cheese, American, 1 slice (2/3 oz)	6
Cottage cheese, 1/2 cup	15
Breads, cereals, grains	
Bread, 1 slice	2
Cold cereal, 1 oz	2
Oatmeal, 1/3 cup dry or 2/3 cup cooked	5
Starchy Vegetables*	
Peas, 1/2 cup cooked	2
Carrots, 1/2 cup cooked	2
Corn, 1/2 cup cooked	2
Beets, 1/2 cup cooked	2
Winter squash, 1/2 cup	2
Potato, 1 small	2

* 4 oz cooked = 5–6 oz raw (approx. size of deck of cards)

** Whereas starchy vegetables contribute a little protein, most watery vegetables and fruits offer negligible amounts of protein. They may contribute a total of 5 to 10 grams of protein per day, depending on how much you eat.

Appendix F:

VITAMIN CHART

Vitamin name (Other terms)	RDA for adults age 19-50; Daily Value (DV)	Major Sources
Fat-Soluble Vitamins		
Vitamin A (retinol: provitamin carotenoids) RDA	900 RA (Men) 700 RA (Women) (RAE= Retinol Activity Erquivalents) DV=1,000 RAE	Retinol in animal food; liver, whole milk, fortified milk, cheese. Carotenoids in plant foods: carrots, green leafy vegetables, sweet potatoes, fortified margarine from vegetable oils
Vitamin D (cholecalciferol) AI	200 IU or 5 mcg DV=400 IU	Vitamin-D fortified foods like dairy products and margarine, fish oils; action of sunlight on the skin
Vitamin E (tocopherol)	15 mg d-alpha Tocopherol DV=30 IU	Vegetable oils, margarine, green leafy vegetables, wheat germ, whole-grain products, egg yolks
Vitamin K (phylloquinone; menoquinone)	120 mcg (Men) 90 mcg (Women) DV=80 mcg	Pork and beef liver, eggs, spinach, cauliflower; formation in the human intenstine by bacteria
Water-Soluble Vitamins		
Thiamin (Vitamin B_1)	1.2 mg (Men) 1.1 mg (Women) DV=1.5 mg	Ham, pork, lean meat, liver, whole-grain products, enriched breads and cereals, legumes
Riboflavin (Vitamin B_2)	16 mg (Men) 14 mg (Women) DV=20 mg	Milk and dairy products, meat, eggs, enriched grain products, green leafy vegetables, beans
Niacin (nicotinamide, nicotinic acid)	1.3 mg (Men) 1.1 mg (Women) DV=1.7 mg	Lean meats, fish, poultry, whole-grain products, beans; may be formed in the body from tryptophan, an essential amino acid
Vitamin B_6 (pyridoxal, pyridoxine, pyridoxamine)	1.3 mg DV=2 mg	Protein foods; liver, lean meats, fish poultry, legumes; green leafy vegetables, baked potatoes, bananas

Major Functions in the Body	Deficiency Symptoms	Symptoms of Excessive Consumption
Fat-Soluble Vitamins		
Maintains epithelial tissue in skin and mucous membranes; forms visual purple for night vision; promotes bone development	Night blindness, intestinal infections, impaired growth, xerophthalmia	UL* (Upper Limit) is 3 milligrams/day. Nausea, headache, fatigue, liver and spleen damage, skin peeling, pain in the joints
Acts as a hormone to increase intestinal absorption of calcium and promote bone and tooth formation	Rare; rickets in children and osteomalacia in adults	UL is 50 micrograms/day. Loss of appetite, nausea, irritability, join pain, calcium deposits in soft tissues such as the kidney
Functions as an antioxidant to protect cell membrandes from destruction by oxidation	Extremely rare; disruption of red blood cell membranes; anemia	UL is 1000 milligrams/day. General lack of toxicity with does up to 400 mg. Some reports of headache, fatigue, or diarrhea with megadoses
Essential for blood coagulation processes	Increased bleeding and hemorrhage	No UL set. Possible clot formation (thrombosis), vomiting
Water-Soluble Vitamins		
Serves as a coenzyme for energy production from carbohydrates; essential for normal functioning of the central nervous system	Poor appetite, apathy, mental depression, pain in calf muscles, beriberi	No UL set. General lack of toxicity
Functions as a coenzyme involved in energy production from carbohydrates and fats; maintenance of healthy skin	Dermatitis, cracks at the corners of the mouth, sores on the tongue, damage to the cornea	No UL set. General lack of toxicity
Functions as a coenzyme for the aerobic and anaerobic production of energy from carbohydrate; helps synthesize fat and blocks release of FFA; needed for healthy skin	Loss of appetite, weakness, skin lesions, gastrointestinal problems, pellagra	UL is 35 milligrams/day. Nicotinic acid causes headache, nausea, burning and itching skin, flushing of face, liver damage
Functions as a coenzyme involved in energy production from carbohydrates and fats; maintenance of healthy skin	Nervous irritability, convulsions, dermatitis, sores on tongue, anemia	UL is 100 milligrams/day. Loss of nerve sensation, impaired gait

UL means upper limit.

VITAMIN CHART (continued)

Vitamin name (Other terms)	RDA for adults age 19-50; Daily Value (DV)	Major Sources
Water-Soluble Vitamins (continued)		
Vitamin B₁₂ (cobalamin; cyanoco-balamin)	2.4 mcg DV=6 mcg	Animal foods only: meat, fish, poultry, milk, eggs
Folate (folic acid)	400 DFE (DFE=Dietary Folate Equivalent) DV=400 DFE	Liver, green leafy vegetables, legumes, nuts, fortified cereals
Biotin	30 mcg DV=300 mg	Meats, legumes, milk, egg yolk, whole-grain products, most vegetables
Pantothenic acid	5 mg DV=300 mg	Beef and pork liver, lean meats, milk, eggs, legumes, whole-grain products, most vegetables
Choline	550 mg (Men) 425 mg (Women) DV=none	Milk, liver, eggs, peanuts; found in most foods as part of cell membranes
Vitamin C (ascorbic acid)	90 mg (Men) 75 mg (Women) DV=60 mg	Citrus fruits, green leafy vegetables, broccoli, peppers, strawberries, potatoes

Major Functions in the Body	Deficiency Symptoms	Symptoms of Excessive Consumption
Water-Soluble Vitamins (continued)		
Functions as a coenzyme for formation of DNA, RBC development, and maintenance of nerve tissue	Pernicious anemia, nerve damage resulting in paralysis	No UL* set. General lack of toxicity
Functions as a coenzyme for DNA formation and RBC development	Fatigue, gastrointestinal disorders, diarrhea, anemia, neural tube defects in newborns	UL is 1,000 micrograms/day. May prevent detection of pernicious anemia caused by B_{12} deficiency
Functions as a coenzyme in the metabolism of carbohydrates, fats, and protein	Rare; may be caused by excessive intake of raw egg whites; fatigue, nausea, skin rashes	No UL set. General lack of toxicity
Functions as part of coenzyme A in energy metabolism	Rare; produced only clinically: fatigue, nausea, skin rashes	No UL set. General lack of toxicity
Functions as precursor for lecithin, a phospholipid in cell membranes	Rare; liver damage	UL is 3.5 grams/day. May lead to fishy body odor, gastrointestinal distress, vomiting, low blood pressure
Forms collagen essential for connective tissue development; aids in absorption of iron; helps form epinephrine; serves as antioxidant	Weakness, rough skin, slow wound healing, bleeding gums, scurvy	UL is 2,000 milligrams/day. Diarrhea, possible kidney stones, rebound scurvy

UL means upper limit.

Appendix G:

MACROMINERALS

	Functions	Sources	Cautions
Calcium	Skeletal structure, muscle contraction and relaxation, blood pressure, nerve function, and immune system.	All dairy products, tofu, dark green leafy vegetables, legumes (dried beans and peas, and canned fish (with edible bones).	Poorly developed and deformed skeleton, increased skeletal fragility, and growth stunting in children.
Phosphorus	Present in the cell wall as "phospholipids," involved high energy bonds of energy metabolic processes, and helps to maintain body pH (acidity/alkalinity).	Present in all foods of animal origin, and also present in legumes.	Deficiency is only seen in conjunction with the intake of certain drugs. Calcium deficiency may occur with excess intake of phosphorus.
Potassium	Involved in protein synthesis, water balance, pH balance, nerve impulse transmission, and muscle contraction. The most prevalent intercellular electrolyte.	Present in meats, poultry, dairy products, fruits, vegetables, grains, and legumes. Bananas and oranges are good nonmeat sources.	Deficiency is associated with weakness, paralysis, and confusion, and is commonly seen in conjunction with dehydration. Severe deficiency may cause death.
Sulfur	Part of some amino acids, biotin, thiamin, and insulin. Involved in the shape of some proteins (through sulfur bonding structures). Detoxifies certain substances.	Present in all foods that contain protein (as most foods do).	Deficiency would only occur in the presence of severe protein deprivation (a rare occurence), and toxicity would only occur in the presence of a protein excess (a documented condition in animals but not humans).
Sodium	The major extracellular (blood) electrolyte, involved in fluid balance, pH balance, and nerve impulse transmission.	Present in salt, most fast foods, and in many preserved foods.	Those individuals with sodium sensitivity develop hypertension with excessive intake. A deficiency of sodium leads to muscle cramping, lethargy, and anorexia.
Chloride	Involved in digestive enzymes (hydrochloric acid in the stomach).	Present in table salt (sodium chloride), processed and preserved foods, and fast foods.	Inadequate intake may lead to growth retardation in children, cramps, lethargy, and anorexia.
Magnesium	Involved in bone strength, protein synthesis, muscle contraction, and nerve impulse transmission. The second most prevalent intercellular electrolyte.	Present in nuts, legumes, whole grains, dark green leafy vegetables, seafood, and cocoa.	Inadequate intake may lead to muscle weakness, convulsions, hallucinations, and growth failure. Excess intake (typically through frequent intake of magnesium-containing antacids and laxatives) may lead to kidney problems, confusion, and poor muscular coordination.

Appendix H:

COMPARING FRUITS

Fruit	Amount	Calories	Vitamin A (IU)	Vitamin C (mg)	Potassium (mg)
Apple	1 medium	80	75	10	160
Apple juice	1 cup	115	0	2	300
Apricots	10 halves dried	85	2550	1	480
Banana	1 medium	105	90	10	450
Blueberries, raw	1 cup	80	145	20	260
Cantaloupe	1 cup pieces	55	5160	70	495
Cherries	10 sweet	50	145	5	150
Cranberry juice	1 cup	140	10	90	55
Dates	5 dried	115	20	—	270
Figs	1 medium raw	35	70	1	115
Grapefruit	1/3 medium pink	40	155	45	170
Grapefruit juice	1 cup white	95	25	95	400
Grapes	1 cup	60	90	5	175
Honeydew melon	1 cub cubes	60	70	40	460
Kiwi	1 medium	45	135	75	250
Orange, naval	1 medium	60	240	75	230
Orange juice	1 cup fresh	110	500	125	500
Peach	1 medium	35	465	5	170
Pear	1 medium	100	35	5	210
Pineapple	1 cup raw	75	35	25	175
Pineapple juice	1 cup	140	13	25	335
Prunes	5 dried	100	830	2	310
Raisins	1/3 cup	150	5	2	375
Strawberries	1 cup raw	45	40	85	245
Watermelon	1 cup	50	585	15	185

Appendix I:

EATING DISORDERS

Athletes who have disordered eating tend to have similar personality traits that affect their attitudes toward food, exercise, and weight. The traits may be the result of growing up in a family in which a parent had alcoholism or in an otherwise dysfunctional family in which a parent may have been unavailable for the child. If you find yourself struggling with food and fitting the following description, you should understand that food is not a problem; it's likely a symptom of problems with life. Please talk to a professional.

Characteristic Trait	How commonly expressed
Drive for perfection	"I've exercised for an hour every day for the past two years."
Desire for control	"I never eat out after 7:00 p.m."
Compulsive behavior	"I work out for two hours every day, regardless of injuries, illness, or travel."
Feelings of inadequacy	"I could have biked even faster if I'd lost more weight."
Difficulty having fun	"Thanks for inviting me to the movie. I'll pass—I have to do my workout at the gym."
Trouble with intimate relationships	"My husband gets angry with me for spending two hours every night exercising and absent from my family."

Appendix J:

EXERCISE CALORIES

When using this appendix, keep these points in mind:

1 The figures are approximate and include the resting energy expenditure (REE). Thus, the total cost of the exercise includes not only the energy expended by the exercise itself, but also the amount you would have used anyway during the same period. Suppose you ran for 1 hour and the calculated energy cost was 800 calories. During that same time at rest, your REE may have been 75 calories, so the net cost of the exercise is 735 calories.

2 The figures in the table are only for the time your are performing the activity. For example, in an hour of basketball, you may exercise strenuously only for 35 to 40 minutes, as you may take time-outs and may rest during foul shots. In general record only the amount of time that you are actually exercising during the activity.

3 The energy cost, expressed in **calories per minute**, will vary for different physical activities in a given individual depending on several factors. For example, the caloric cost of bicycling will vary depending on the type of bicycle, going uphill and downhill, and wind resistance. Walking with hand weights or ankle weights will increase energy output. Energy cost for swimming at a certain pace will depend of swimming efficiency, so the less efficient swimmer will expend more calories. Thus, the values expressed here are approximations and may be increased or decreased depending upon various factors that influence energy cost for a specific physical activity.

4 Not all body weights could be listed, but you may approximate by using the closest weight listed.

5 There may be small differences between males and females, but not enough to make a significant difference in the total caloric value for most exercises. *(Williams)*

Body weight

Kilograms	48	48	50	52	55	57	59	61	64	66	68	70	73	75
Pounds	100	105	110	115	120	125	130	135	140	145	150	155	160	165

Sedentary activities (calories per minute)

Lying quietly	1.0	1.0	1.1	1.1	1.2	1.3	1.3	1.4	1.4	1.5	1.5	1.5	1.6	1.6
Sitting and writing, card playing, etc.	1.2	1.3	1.4	1.5	1.5	1.6	1.7	1.7	1.8	1.8	1.9	2.0	2.0	2.1
Standing with light work,cleaning, etc.	2.7	2.9	3.0	3.1	3.3	3.4	3.5	3.7	3.8	3.9	4.1	4.2	4.4	4.5

Physical activities (calories per minute)

Archery	3.1	3.3	3.5	3.6	3.8	4.0	4.1	4.3	4.5	4.6	4.8	4.9	5.1	5.3
Baseball														
Player	3.1	3.3	3.4	3.6	3.8	4.0	4.1	4.3	4.4	4.5	4.7	4.8	5.0	5.2
Pitcher	3.9	4.1	4.3	4.5	4.7	4.9	5.1	5.3	5.5	5.7	5.9	6.0	6.3	6.5
Basketball														
Half court	3.0	3.1	3.3	3.5	3.6	3.8	3.9	4.1	4.2	4.4	4.5	4.7	4.8	5.0
Recreational	4.9	5.2	5.5	5.7	6.0	6.2	6.5	6.7	7.0	7.2	7.5	7.7	8.0	8.2
Vigorous competition	6.5	6.8	7.2	7.5	7.8	8.2	8.5	8.8	9.2	9.5	9.9	10.2	10.5	10.9
Bicycling, level														
(mph) (min/mile)														
5 12:00	1.9	2.0	2.1	2.2	2.3	2.4	2.5	2.6	2.7	2.8	2.9	3.0	3.1	3.2
10 6:00	4.2	4.4	4.6	4.8	5.1	5.3	5.5	5.7	5.9	6.1	6.4	6.6	6.8	7.0
15 4:00	7.3	7.6	8.0	8.4	8.7	9.1	9.5	9.8	10.0	10.5	10.9	11.3	11.6	12.0
20 3:00	10.7	11.2	11.7	12.3	12.8	13.3	13.9	14.4	14.9	15.5	16.0	16.5	17.1	17.6
Bowling	2.7	2.8	3.0	3.1	3.3	3.4	3.5	3.7	3.8	3.9	4.1	4.2	4.4	4.5
Dancing														
Moderately (waltz)	3.1	3.3	3.5	3.6	3.8	4.0	4.1	4.3	4.5	4.6	4.8	4.9	5.1	5.3
Active (square, disco)	4.5	4.7	5.0	5.2	5.4	5.6	5.9	6.1	6.3	6.6	6.8	7.0	7.3	7.5
Aerobic (vigorously)	6.0	6.3	6.7	7.0	7.3	7.6	7.9	8.2	8.5	8.8	9.1	9.4	9.7	10.0
Fencing														
Moderately	3.0	0.5	3.6	3.8	4.0	4.1	4.3	4.5	4.6	4.8	5.0	5.2	5.3	5.5
Vigorously	6.6	7.0	7.3	7.7	8.0	8.3	8.7	9.0	9.4	9.7	10.0	10.4	10.7	11.0
Football														
Moderate	3.3	3..5	3.6	3.8	4.0	4.1	4.3	4.5	4.6	4.8	5.0	5.2	5.3	5.5
Touch, vigorous5.5	5.8	6.1	6.4	6.6	6.9	7.2	7.5	7.8	8.0	8.3	8.6	8.9	9.2	
Golf														
2-some (carry clubs)	3.6	3.8	4.0	4.2	4.4	4.6	4.7	4.9	5.1	5.3	5.4	5.6	5.8	6.0
4-some (carry clubs)	2.7	2.9	3.0	3.1	3.3	3.4	3.5	3.7	3.8	3.9	4.1	4.2	4.4	4.5
Power-cart	1.9	2.0	2.1	2.2	2.3	2.4	2.5	2.6	2.7	2.8	2.9	3.0	3.1	3.2
Handball														
Moderate	6.5	6.8	7.2	7.5	7.8	8.2	8.5	8.8	9.2	9.5	9.9	10.2	10.5	10.9
Competitive	7.7	8.0	8.4	8.8	9.2	9.6	10.0	10.4	10.8	11.1	11.5	11.9	12.3	12.7
Hiking, pack (3 mph)	4.5	4.7	5.0	5.2	5.4	5.6	5.9	6.1	6.3	6.6	6.8	7.0	7.3	7.5
Hockey, field	5.0	6.3	6.7	7.0	7.3	7.6	7.9	8.2	8.5	8.8	9.1	9.4	9.7	10.0
Hockey, ice	6.6	7.0	7.3	7.7	8.0	8.3	8.7	9.0	9.4	9.7	10.0	10.4	10.7	11.0
Horseback riding														
Posting to trot	4.2	4.4	4.6	4.8	5.1	5.3	5.5	5.7	5.9	6.1	6.4	6.6	6.8	7.0
Gallop	5.7	6.0	6.3	6.6	6.9	7.2	7.5	7.8	8.1	8.4	8.7	9.0	9.3	9.5
Jogging (see running)														

Body weight

Kilos	77	80	82	84	86	89	91	93	95	98	100	102	104	107	109	111	113
Lbs	170	175	180	185	190	195	200	205	210	215	220	225	230	235	240	245	250

Sedentary activities (calories per minute)

1.7	1.7	1.8	1.8	1.9	1.9	2.0	2.0	2.1	2.1	2.2	2.2	2.3	2.3	2.4	2.4	2.5
2.2	2.2	2.3	2.4	2.4	2.5	2.5	2.6	2.7	2.7	2.8	2.8	2.9	3.0	3.0	3.1	3.1
4.6	4.8	4.9	5.0	5.2	5.3	5.4	5.6	5.7	5.9	6.0	6.2	6.3	6.4	6.6	6.7	6.8

Physical activities (calories per minute)

5.4	5.6	5.7	5.9	6.0	6.2	6.4	6.5	6.7	6.9	7.0	7.2	7.4	7.5	7.7	7.9	8.0
5.3	5.5	5.6	5.8	5.9	6.1	6.4	6.5	6.7	6.9	7.0	7.2	7.4	7.5	7.6	7.8	7.9
6.7	6.9	7.1	7.3	7.4	7.7	7.9	8.0	8.2	8.5	8.6	8.8	9.0	9.1	9.3	9.5	9.6
5.1	5.3	5.4	5.6	5.7	5.9	6.0	6.2	6.4	6.5	6.7	6.9	7.0	7.2	7.3	7.5	7.7
8.5	8.7	9.0	9.2	9.5	9.7	10.0	10.2	10.5	10.7	11.0	11.2	11.5	11..7	12.0	12.2	12.5
11.2	11.5	11.9	12.2	12.5	12.9	13.2	13.5	13.8	14.2	14.5	14.9	15.2	15.5	15.9	16.2	16.5
3.3	3.4	3.5	3.6	3.7	3.8	3.9	4.0	4.1	4.2	4.3	4.4	4.5	4.6	4.7	4.8	4.9
7.2	7.4	7.6	7.9	8.1	8.3	8.5	8.7	8.9	9.1	9.4	9.6	9.8	10.0	10.2	10.4	10.6
12.4	12.7	13.1	13.4	13.8	14.2	14.5	14.9	15.3	15.6	16.0	16.4	16..7	17.1	17.5	17.8	18.2
18.1	18.7	19.2	19.7	20.3	20.8	21.3	21.9	22.4	22.9	23.5	24.0	24.5	25.1	25.6	26.1	26.7
4.6	4.8	4.9	5.0	5.2	5.3	5.5	5.6	5.7	5.9	6.0	6.1	6.3	6.4	6.5	6.7	6.8
5.4	5.6	5.7	5.9	6.0	6.2	6.4	6.5	6.7	6.9	7.0	7.1	7.3	7.5	7.8	8.1	8.3
7.7	7.9	8.2	8.4	8.6	8.9	9.1	9.3	9.5	9.8	10.0	10.2	10.5	10.7	10.9	11.2	11.4
10.3	10.6	10.9	11.2	11.5	11.8	12.1	12.4	12.7	13.0	13.3	13.6	13.9	14.2	14.5	14.8	15.1
5.7	5.8	6.0	6.2	6.3	6.5	6.7	6.8	7.0	7.1	7.3	7.5	7.6	7.8	8.0	8.1	8.3
11.4	11.7	12.1	12.4	12.7	13.1	13.4	13.8	14.1	14.4	14.8	15.1	15.4	15.8	16.1	16.4	16.8
5.7	5.8	6.0	6.2	6.3	6.5	6.7	6.8	7.0	7.1	7.3	7.5	7.6	7.8	8.0	8.1	8.3
9.4	9.7	10.0	10.3	10.6	10.8	11.1	11.4	11.7	12.0	12.2	12.5	12.8	13.1	13.3	13.6	13.9
6.2	6.4	6.6	6.7	6.9	7.1	7.3	7.4	7.6	7.8	8.0	8.1	8.3	8.5	8.7	8.8	9.0
4.6	4.8	4.9	5.0	5.2	5.3	5.4	5.6	5.7	5.9	6.0	6.2	6.3	6.5	6.6	6.8	6.9
3.3	3.4	3.5	3.6	3.7	3.8	3.9	4.0	4.1	4.2	4.3	4.4	4.5	4.6	4.7	4.8	4.9
11.2	11.5	11.9	12.2	12.5	12.9	13.2	13.5	13.8	14.2	14.5	14.8	15.1	15.5	15.8	16.1	16.5
13.1	13.5	13.9	14.3	14.7	15.0	15.4	15.8	16.2	16.6	17.0	17.4	17.8	18.2	18.6	19.0	19.4
7.7	7.9	8.2	8.4	8.6	8.9	9.1	9.3	9.5	9.8	10.0	10.2	10.5	10.7	10.9	11.2	11.4
10.3	10.6	10.9	11.2	11.5	11.8	12.1	12.4	12.7	13.0	13.3	13.6	13.9	14.2	14.5	14.8	15.1
11.4	11.7	12.1	12.4	12.7	13.1	13.4	13.8	14.1	14.4	14.8	15.1	15.4	15.8	16.1	16.5	16.8
7.2	7.4	7.6	7.9	8..1	8.3	8.5	8.7	8.9	9.1	9.4	9.6	9.8	10.0	10.2	10.4	10.7
9.8	10.1	10.4	10.7	11.0	11.3	11.6	11.9	12.2	12.5	12.8	13.1	13.4	13.7	14.0	14.3	14.6

Body weight

Kilograms	48	48	50	52	55	57	59	61	64	66	68	70	73	75
Pounds	100	105	110	115	120	125	130	135	140	145	150	155	160	165

Physical activities (continued) (calories per minute)

Judo	8.5	8.9	9.3	9.8	10.2	10.6	11.0	11.5	11.9	12.3	12.8	13.2	13.6	14.1
Karate	8.5	8.9	9.3	9.8	10.2	10.6	11.0	11.5	11.9	12.3	12.8	13.2	13.6	14.1
Mountain climbing	6.5	6.8	7.2	7.5	7.8	8.2	8.5	8.8	9.2	9.5	9.8	10.2	10.5	10.8
Raquetball	6.5	6.8	7.1	7.5	7.8	8.1	8.4	8.8	9.1	9.4	9.8	10.1	10.4	10.7
Roller Skating (9 mph)	4.2	4.4	4.6	4.8	5.1	5.3	5.5	5.7	5.9	6.1	6.4	6.6	6.8	7.0
Running (steady rate)														
(mph) (min/mile)														
5.0 12:00	6.0	6.3	6.6	7.0	7.3	7.6	7.9	8.2	8.5	8.8	9.1	9.4	9.7	10.0
5.5 10:55	6.7	7.0	7.3	7.7	8.0	8.4	8.7	9.0	9.4	9.7	10.0	10.4	10.7	11.1
6.0 10:00	7.2	7.6	8.0	8.4	8.7	9.1	9.5	9.8	10.2	10.6	10.9	11.3	11.7	12.0
7.0 8:35	8.5	8.9	9.3	9.8	10.2	10.6	11.0	11.5	11.9	12.3	12.8	13.2	13.6	14.1
8.0 7:30	9.7	10.2	10.7	11.2	11.6	12.1	12.6	13.1	13.6	14.1	14.6	15.1	15.6	16.1
9.0 6:40	10.8	11.3	11.9	12.4	12.9	13.5	14.0	14.6	15.1	15.7	16.2	16.8	17.3	17.9
10.0 6:00	12.1	12.7	13.3	13.9	14.5	15.1	15.7	16.4	17.0	17.6	18.2	18.8	19.4	20.0
11.0 5:28	13.3	14.0	14.6	15.3	16.0	16.7	17.3	18.0	18.7	19.4	20.0	20.7	21.4	22.1
12.0 5:00	14.5	15.2	16.0	16.7	17.4	18.2	18.9	19.7	20.4	21.1	21.9	22.6	23.3	24.1
Skating, ice (9 mph)	4.2	4.4	4.6	4.8	5.1	5.2	5.5	5.7	5.9	6.1	6.4	6.6	6.8	7.0
Skating, in line (13mph)	9.5	10.0	10.5	10.9	11.5	12.0	12.4	12.8	13.4	13.9	14.3	14.7	15.3	15.7
Skiing, cross-country														
(mph) (min/mile)														
2.5 24:00	5.0	5.2	5.5	5.7	6.0	6.2	6.5	6.7	7.0	7.2	7.5	7.8	8.0	8.3
4.0 15:00	6.5	6.8	7.2	7.5	7.8	8.2	8.5	8.8	9.2	9.5	9.9	10.2	10.5	10.9
5.0 12:00	7.7	8.0	8.4	8.8	9.2	9.6	10.0	10.4	10.8	11.1	11.5	11.9	12.3	12.7
Skiing, downhill	6.5	6.8	7.2	7.5	7.8	8.2	8.5	8.8	9.2	9.5	9.9	10.2	10.5	10.9
Soccer	5.9	6.2	6.6	6.9	7.2	7.5	7.8	8.1	8.4	8.7	9.0	9.3	9.6	9.9
Squash														
Normal	6.7	7.0	7.3	7.7	8.0	8.4	8.7	9.1	9.5	9.8	10.1	10.5	10.8	11.2
Competition	7.7	8.0	8.4	0.0	0.2	0.6	10.0	10.4	10.8	11.1	11.5	11.9	12.3	12.7
Swimming (yards/min)														
Backstroke														
25	2.5	2.6	2.8	2.9	3.0	3.1	3.3	3.4	3.5	3.7	3.8	3.9	4.0	4.2
30	3.5	3.7	3.9	4.1	4.2	4.4	4.6	4.8	4.9	5.1	5.3	5.5	5.6	5.8
35	4.5	4.7	5.0	5.2	5.4	5.6	5.9	6.1	6.3	6.6	6.8	7.0	7.3	7.5
40	5.5	5.8	6.1	6.4	6.6	6.9	7.2	7.5	7.8	8.0	8.3	8.6	8.9	9.2
Breaststroke														
20	3.1	3.3	3.5	3.6	3.8	4.0	4.1	4.3	4.5	4.6	4.8	4.9	5.1	5.3
30	4.7	5.0	5.2	5.4	5.7	5.9	6.2	6.4	6.7	6.9	7.1	7.4	7.6	7.9
40	6.3	6.7	7.0	7.3	7.6	8.0	8.3	8.6	8.9	9.3	9.6	9.9	10.2	10.5
Front crawl														
20	3.1	3.3	3.5	3.6	3.8	4.0	4.1	4.3	4.5	4.6	4.8	4.9	5.1	5.3
25	4.0	4.2	4.4	4.6	4.8	5.0	5.2	5.4	5.6	5.8	6.0	6.2	6.4	6.6
35	4.8	5.1	5.4	5.6	5.9	6.1	6.4	6.6	6.8	7.0	7.3	7.5	7.8	8.0
45	5.7	6.0	6.3	6.6	6.9	7.2	7.5	7.8	8.1	8.4	8.7	9.0	9.3	9.5
50	7.0	7.4	7.7	8.1	8.5	8.8	9.2	9.5	9.9	10.3	10.6	11.0	11.3	11.7
Table tennis	3.4	3.6	3.8	4.0	4.1	4.3	4.5	4.7	4.8	5.0	5.2	5.4	5.5	5.7

Body weight

Kilos	77	80	82	84	86	89	91	93	95	98	100	102	104	107	109	111	113
Lbs	170	175	180	185	190	195	200	205	210	215	220	225	230	235	240	245	250

Physical activities (continued) (calories per minute)

14.5	14.9	15.4	15.8	16.2	16.6	17.1	17.5	17.9	18.4	18.8	19.2	19.6	20.1	20.5	20.9	30.4
14.5	14.9	15.4	15.8	16.2	16.6	17.1	17.5	17.9	18.4	18.8	19.2	19.6	20.1	20.5	20.9	30.4
11.2	11.5	11.8	12.1	12.5	12.8	13.1	13.5	13.8	14.1	14.5	14.8	15.1	15.5	15.8	16.1	16.5
11.1	11.4	11.7	12.0	12.4	12.7	13.0	13.4	13.7	14.0	14.4	14.7	15.0	15.4	15.7	16.0	16.4
7.2	7.4	7.6	7.9	8.1	8.3	8.5	8.7	8.9	9.1	9.4	9.6	9.8	10.0	10.3	10.5	10.7
10.3	10.6	10.9	11.2	11.6	11.9	12.2	12.5	12.8	13.1	13.4	13.7	14.0	14.3	14.6	14.9	15.2
11.4	11.7	12.1	12.4	12.8	13.1	13.4	13.8	14.1	14.5	14.8	15.2	15.5	15.8	16.1	16.4	16.8
12.4	12.8	13.1	13.5	13.8	14.3	14.6	15.0	15.4	15.7	16.1	16.4	16.8	17.3	17.6	18.0	18.3
14.5	14.9	15.4	15.8	16.2	16.6	17.1	17.5	17.9	18.4	18.8	19.2	19.6	20.1	20.5	20.9	30.4
16.6	17.1	17.6	18.1	18.5	19.0	19.5	20.0	20.5	21.0	21.5	22.0	22.5	23.0	23.5	24.0	24.5
18.4	19.0	19.5	20.1	20.6	21.2	21.7	22.2	22.8	23.3	23.9	24.4	25.0	25.5	26.1	26.6	27.2
20.7	21.3	21.9	22.5	23.1	23.7	24.2	24.8	25.4	26.0	26.7	27.3	27.9	28.5	29.1	29.7	30.3
22.7	23.4	24.1	24.8	25.4	26.1	26.8	27.5	28.1	28.8	29.5	30.2	31.0	31.7	32.4	33.1	33.9
24.8	25.6	26.3	27.0	27.8	28.5	29.2	30.0	30.7	31.5	32.2	33.0	33.8	34.5	35.3	36.0	36.8
7.2	7.4	7.6	7.9	8.1	8.3	8.5	8.7	8.9	9.1	9.4	9.6	9.8	10.0	10.2	10.5	10.7
16.2	16.8	17.2	17.6	18.1	18.7	19.1	19.5	20.0	20.6	21.0	21.4	22.0	22.5	23.1	23.5	24.0
8.5	8.8	9.0	9.3	9.5	9.8	10.0	10.3	10.6	10.8	11.1	11.3	11.6	11.8	12.1	12.3	12.6
11.2	11.5	11.9	12.2	12.5	12.9	13.2	13.5	13.8	14.2	14.5	14.8	15.1	15.5	15.8	16.1	16.5
13.1	13.5	13.9	14.3	14.7	15.0	15.4	15.8	16.2	16.6	17.0	17.3	17.7	18.1	18.5	18.9	19.3
11.2	11.5	11.9	12.2	12.5	12.9	13.2	13.5	13.8	14.2	14.5	14.8	15.1	15.5	15.8	16.1	16.4
10.2	10.5	10.8	11.1	11.4	11.7	12.0	12.3	12.6	12.9	13.2	13.5	13.8	14.1	14.4	14.7	15.0
11.5	11.8	12.2	12.5	12.9	13.2	13.5	13.9	14.2	14.6	14.9	15.3	15.6	16.0	16.3	169.7	17.0
13.1	13.5	13.9	14.3	14.7	15.0	15.4	15.8	16.2	16.6	17.0	17.3	17.7	18.1	18.5	18.9	19.2
4.3	4.4	4.5	4.7	4.8	4.9	5.1	5.2	5.3	5.4	5.6	5.7	5.9	6.0	6.1	6.2	6.3
6.0	6.2	6.4	6.5	6.7	6.9	7.1	7.2	7.4	7.6	7.8	7.9	8.1	8.3	8.5	8.7	8.9
7.7	7.9	8.2	8.4	8.6	8.9	9.1	9.3	9.5	9.8	10.0	10.2	10.4	10.7	10.9	11.1	11.3
9.4	9.7	10.0	10.3	10.6	10.8	11.1	11.4	11.7	12.0	12.2	12.5	12.8	13.1	13.4	13.6	13.9
5.4	5.6	5.7	5.9	6.0	6.2	6.4	6.5	6.7	6.9	7.0	7.2	7.4	7.5	7.7	7.9	8.0
8.1	8.3	8.6	8.8	9.1	9.3	9.5	9.8	10.0	10.3	10.5	10.8	11.0	11.2	11.5	11.7	12.0
10.9	11.2	11.5	11.9	12.2	12.5	12.8	13.1	13.5	13.8	14.1	14.4	14.7	15.1	15.4	15.7	16.0
5.4	5.6	5.7	5.9	6.0	6.2	6.4	6.5	6.7	6.9	7.0	7.2	7.4	7.5	7.7	7.9	8.0
6.8	7.0	7.2	7.4	7.6	7.8	8.0	8.2	8.4	8.6	8.8	9.0	9.2	9.4	9.6	9.8	10.0
8.3	8.5	8.8	9.0	9.2	9.4	9.7	9.9	10.2	10.4	10.7	10.9	11.2	11.4	11.7	11.9	12.2
9.8	10.1	10.4	10.7	11.0	11.3	11.6	11.9	12.2	12.5	12.8	13.1	13.4	13.7	14.0	14.3	14.6
12.0	12.4	12.8	13.1	13.5	13.8	14.2	14.5	14.9	15.2	15.6	15.9	16.3	16.6	17.0	17.3	17.7
5.9	6.1	6.3	6.4	6.6	6.8	7.0	7.1	7.3	7.5	7.7	7.8	8.0	8.2	8.4	8.5	8.7

Body weight

		48	48	50	52	55	57	59	61	64	66	68	70	73	75
Kilograms		48	48	50	52	55	57	59	61	64	66	68	70	73	75
Pounds		100	105	110	115	120	125	130	135	140	145	150	155	160	165

Physical activities (continued) (calories per minute)

		48/100	48/105	50/110	52/115	55/120	57/125	59/130	61/135	64/140	66/145	68/150	70/155	73/160	75/165
Tennis															
Singles, recreational		5.0	5.2	5.5	5.7	6.0	6.2	6.5	6.7	7.0	7.2	7.5	7.8	8.0	8.3
Doubles, recreational		3.4	3.6	3.8	4.0	4.1	4.3	4.5	4.7	4.8	5.0	5.2	5.4	5.5	5.7
Competition		6.4	6.7	7.1	7.4	7.7	8.1	8.4	8.7	9.1	9.4	9.8	10.1	10.4	10.8
Volleyball															
Moderate, recreational		2.9	3.0	3.2	3.3	3.5	3.6	3.8	3.9	4.1	4.2	4.4	4.5	4.7	4.8
Vigorous, competition		6.5	6.8	7.1	7.5	7.8	8.1	8.4	8.8	9.1	9.4	9.8	10.1	10.4	10.7
Walking															
(mph)	(min/mile)														
1.0	60:00	1.5	1.6	1.7	1.8	1.8	1.9	2.0	2.1	2.2	2.2	2.3	2.4	2.4	2.5
2.0	30:00	2.1	2.2	2.3	2.4	2.5	2.6	2.8	2.9	3.0	3.1	3.2	3.3	3.4	3.5
2.3	26:00	2.3	2.4	2.5	2.7	2.8	2.9	3.0	3.1	3.2	3.4	3.5	3.6	3.7	3.8
3.0	20:00	2.7	2.9	3.0	3.1	3.3	3.4	3.5	3.7	3.8	3.9	4.1	4.2	4.4	4.5
3.2	18.45	3.1	3.3	3.4	3.6	3.8	4.0	4.1	4.3	4.4	4.5	4.7	4.8	5.0	5.2
3.5	17.10	3.3	3.5	3.7	3.9	4.0	4.2	4.4	4.6	4.7	4.9	5.1	5.3	5.4	5.6
4.0	15:00	4.2	4.4	4.6	4.8	5.1	5.3	5.5	5.7	5.9	6.1	6.4	6.6	6.8	7.0
4.5	13:20	4.7	5.0	5.2	5.4	5.7	5.9	6.2	6.4	6.7	6.9	7.1	7.4	7.6	7.9
5.0	12:00	5.4	5.7	6.0	6.3	6.5	6.8	7.1	7.4	7.7	7.9	8.2	8.4	8.7	9.0
5.4	11:00	6.2	6.6	6.9	7.2	7.5	7.9	8.2	8.5	8.8	9.2	9.5	9.8	10.1	10.4
5.8	10:20	7.7	8.0	8.4	8.8	9.2	9.6	10.0	10.4	10.8	11.1	11.5	11.9	12.3	12.7
Water Skiing		5.0	5.2	5.5	5.7	6.0	6.2	6.5	6.7	7.0	7.2	7.5	7.8	8.0	8.3
Weight Training		5.2	5.4	5.7	6.0	6.2	6.5	6.8	7.0	7.3	7.6	7.8	8.1	8.3	8.6
Wrestling		8.5	8.9	9.3	9.8	10.2	10.6	11.0	11.5	11.9	12.3	12.8	13.2	13.6	14.1

Body weight

Kilos	77	80	82	84	86	89	91	93	95	98	100	102	104	107	109	111	113
Lbs	170	175	180	185	190	195	200	205	210	215	220	225	230	235	240	245	250

Physical activities (continued) (calories per minute)

8.5	8.8	9.0	9.3	9.5	9.8	10.0	10.3	10.6	10.8	11.1	11.3	11.6	11.8	12.1	12.3	12.6
5.9	6.1	6.3	6.4	6.6	6.8	7.0	7.1	7.3	7.5	7.7	7.8	8.0	8.2	8.4	8.5	8.7
11.1	11.4	11.8	12.1	12.4	12.8	13.1	13.4	13.7	14.1	14.4	14.7	15.0	15.3	15.7	16.0	16.3
5.0	5.1	5.3	5.4	5.6	5.7	5.9	6.0	6.1	6.3	6.4	6.6	6.7	6.9	7.0	7.2	7.3
11.1	11.4	11.7	12.0	12.4	12.7	13.0	13.4	13.7	14.0	14.4	14.7	15.0	15.4	15.7	16.0	16.3
2.6	2.7	2.8	2.9	2.9	3.0	3.1	3.2	3.2	3.3	3.4	3.5	3.5	3.6	3.7	3.8	3.8
3.6	3.7	3.9	4.0	4.1	4.2	4.3	4.4	4.5	4.6	4.7	4.9	5.0	5.1	5.2	5.3	5.4
4.0	4.1	4.2	4.3	4.4	4.5	4.7	4.8	4.9	5.0	5.1	5.2	5.4	5.5	5.6	5.7	5.8
4.6	4.8	4.9	5.0	5.2	5.3	5.4	5.6	5.7	5.9	6.0	6.1	6.3	6.4	6.6	6.7	6.8
5.3	5.5	5.6	5.8	5.9	6.1	6.3	6.4	6.6	6.8	6.9	7.1	7.3	7.4	7.6	7.8	7.9
5.8	6.0	6.2	6.3	6.5	6.7	6.9	7.0	7.2	7.4	7.6	7.7	7.9	8.1	8.3	8.4	8.6
7.2	7.4	7.6	7.9	8.1	8.3	8.5	8.7	8.9	9.1	9.4	9.6	9.8	10.0	10.2	10.5	10.7
8.1	8.3	8.6	8.8	9.1	9.3	9.5	9.8	10.0	10.3	10.5	10.7	11.0	11.2	11.4	11.7	11..9
9.2	9.5	9.8	10.1	10.4	10.6	10.9	11.2	11.5	11.8	12.0	12.3	12.6	12.9	13.1	13.4	13.7
10.8	11.1	11.4	11.8	12.1	12.4	12.7	13.0	13.4	13.7	14.0	14.3	14.6	15.0	15.3	15.6	15.9
13.1	13.5	13.9	14.3	14.7	15.0	15.4	15.8	16.2	16.6	17.0	17.3	17.7	18.1	18.5	18.9	19.2
8.5	8.8	9.0	9.3	9.5	9.8	10.0	10.3	10.6	10.8	11.1	11.3	11.6	11.8	12.1	12.3	12.6
8.9	9.1	9.4	9.7	9.9	10.2	10.5	10.7	11.0	11.2	11.5	11.8	12.0	12.3	12.6	12.8	13.1
14.5	14.9	15.4	15.8	16.2	16.6	17.1	17.5	17.9	18.4	18.8	19.2	19.7	20.1	20.5	21.0	21.4

Appendix K:

UNDERSTANDING PORTIONS

One "rule of thumb" for knowing the right amounts is the "Rule of the Fist." It says that if your food portion is larger than your fist, you may be eating too much. This works in some cases—but not if you're small and carry paws the size of King Kong's. Besides fist-sized servings, this page can help you look at a meal and guesstimate how many grams/calories you're about to eat.

Fast-food chicken salad
⅔ chicken breast

25g carbohydrate (100 cal)
6g fat (54 cal)
20g protein (180 cal)

2 slices whole wheat bread
2 oz. ham
½ cup cottage cheese
1 apple

55g carbohydrate (220 cal)
10g fat (90 cal)
20g protein (80 cal)

1 average slice pizza

30g carbohydrate (120 cal)
12g fat (108 cal)
7g protein (28 cal)

2 Tbs. peanut butter
5 celery sticks (6" long)

20g carbohydrate (80 cal)
15g fat (135 cal)
8g protein (32 cal)

Turkey sandwich
⅓ cup carrots
2 slices white bread
½ cup grapes
2 oz. turkey

45g carbohydrate (180 cal)
7g fat (63 cal)
20g protein (80 cal)

1 cup whole grain cereal
½ cup milk

35g carbohydrate (140 cal)
3g fat (27 cal)
10g protein (40 cal)

Ham, cheese, tomato
sandwich on sourdough
bread

35g carbohydrate (140 cal)
8g fat (72 cal)
14g protein (56 cal)

1 chicken breast
1 egg
1 cup romaine lettuce

15g carbohydrate (60 cal)
5g fat (45 cal)
32g protein (128 cal)

1 cup pork stir fry

18g carbohydrate (72 cal)
10g fat   (90 cal)
15g protein (60 cal)

SPORTS NUTRITION HANDBOOK

Appendix L:

THE FOOD LABEL AT A GLANCE

The food label contains an up-to-date, easy-to-use nutrition information guide and is required on almost all packaged foods. The guide will help people plan a healthy diet. Here is a sample.

Serving sizes are now more consistent across product lines, are stated in both household and metric measures, and reflect the amounts people actually eat.

The list of nutrients covers those most important to the health of today's consumers, most of whom need to worry about getting too much of certain items, such as fat, rather than too few vitamins or minerals, as in the past.

Nutrition Facts

Serving Size 1/2 cup (122g)

Amount Per Serving	As Served
Calories 40	Calories from Fat 5

	% Daily Value
Total Fat 0.5g	1%
Saturated Fat 0g	0%
Cholesterol 0g	0%
Sodium 5mg	0%
Total Carbohydrate 9g	3%
Dietary Fiber 5g	21%
Sugars 4g	
Protein 2g	

Vitamin A 300%	•	Vitamin C 10%
Calcium 2%	•	Iron 4%

Percent Daily Values are based on a 2,000 calorie diet. Your daily values may be higher or lower depending on your calorie needs:

	Calories	2,000	2,500
Total Fat	Less than	65g	80g
Sat Fat	Less than	20g	80g
Cholesterol	Less than	300mg	300mg
Sodium	Less than	2,400mg	2,400mg
Total Carbohydrate		300g	375g
Dietary Fiber		25g	30g

Calories from fat are now shown on the label to help consumers follow dietary guidelines that recommend people get no more than 30% of their calories from fat.

% Daily Value shows how a food fits into the overall daily diet.

Daily Values are based on a daily diet of 2,000 and 2,500 calories. Some daily values show maximums, such as with fat (65 g or less), and others are minimums, as with carbohydrates (300 g or more). Individuals should adjust the values to fit their own calorie intake.

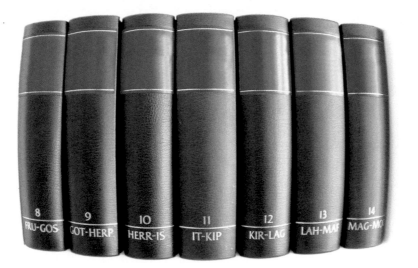

References

Applegate, E. 1999. Effective Nutritional ergogenic aids. *International Journal of Sport Nutrition* 9:229-89.

Applegate, L. 2002. *Encyclopedia of Sports and Fitness Nutrition.* Prima Publishing, Roseville, CA

Armstrong, L. 2002. Caffeine, body fluid-electrolyte balance, and exercise performance. *International Journal of Sport Nutrition and Exercise Metabolism* 12:189-206.

Baar, S.I. 1999. Effects of dehydration on exercise performance. *Canadian Journal of Applied Physiology* 24:164-72.

Bahrke, M.S., and Morgan, W.P. 1994. Evaluation of the ergogenic properties of ginseng. *Sports Medicine* 18:229- 48.

Beard, J., and Tobin, B. 2000. Iron Status and exercise. *American Journal of Clinical Nutrition.* 72:594S-97S.

Benardot, D. *Sports Nutrition for Serious Athletes,* Human Kinetics, Champaign, IL. ©2000

Blomstrand, E. 2001. Amino acids and central fatigue. *Amino Acids* 20:25-34.

Blomstrand, E., et al. 1997. Influence of ingesting a solution of branched-chain amino acids on perceived exertion during exercise. *Acta Physiologica Scandinavia* 159:41-49.

Bonci, L. 2002. Energy drinks: Help, harm, or hype? *Sports Science Exchange* 15 (1):1-4.

Bremner, K., et al. 2002. The effect of phosphate loading on erythrocyte 2,3-bisphosphoglycerate levels. *Clinical Chimica Acta* 323:111-14.

Brilla, L., and Gunter, K., 1994. Magnesium ameliorates aerobic contribution at high intensity. *Medicine and Science in Sports and Exercise* 26:S53.

Brown, K., et. Al. 2002. Effect of supplemental zinc on the growth and serum zinc concentrations of prepubertal children. A meta-analysis of randomized control trials. *American Journal of Clinical Nutrition* 75:1062-71.

Bucci, L. 1993. *Nutrients as Ergogenic Aids for Sports and Exercise.* Boca Raton, FL: CRC Press.

Bucci, L., et al. 1992. Ornithine supplementation and insulin release in body-builders. *International Journal of Sports Nutrition* 2:287-91.

Budgett, R., et al. 1998. The overtraining syndrome. In *Oxford Textbook of Sports Medicine,* eds. M. Harries, et al. Oxford: Oxford University Press.

Bulow, J. 1993. Lipid metabolism and utilization. In *Principles of Exercise Biochemistry,* ed. J. Poortmans. Basel, Switzerland: Karger.

Burke, R. 2002. Selenium, an antioxidant nutrient. *Nutrition in Clinical Care* 5:75-79.

Burke, E. 2003. *Optimal Muscle Performance and Recovery.* Penguin Putnam Inc. New York, NY.

Burke, L. 2001. Nutritional practices of male female endurance cyclists. *Sports Medicine* 31:521-32.

Cade, R., et al. 1984. Effects of phosphate loading on 2,3-diphosphoglycerate and maximal oxygen uptake. *Medicine and Science in Sports and Exercise* 16:263-68.

Casey, A., et al. 1996. Creatine ingestion favorably affects performance and muscle metabolism during maximal exercise in humans. *American Journal of Physiology* 271:E31-E37.

Cheuvront, S.N. 1999. The zone diet and athletic performance. *Sports Medicine* 27:213-28.

Clark, N. 2003. Nancy Clark's Sports Nutrition Guidebook. Human Kinetics, Champaign IL.

Clark, N. , Tobin, J., Jr. And Ellis, C. 1992. Feeding the ultraendurance athlete: Practical tips and a case study. J. Am. Diet. Assoc. 92 (10): 1258-1262.

Colombani, P.C. 1999. Metabolic effects of a protein-supplemented carbohydrate drink in marathon runners. *International Journal of Sport Nutrition* 9:181-201.

Constantini, N. W., et al. 2000. Iron status of highly active adolescents: Evidence of depleted stores in gymnasts. *International Journal of Sport Nutrition and Exercise Metabolism* 10:62-70. Consumers Union. 2001. Sports supplement dangers. Consumer Reports 66 (6):40-42.

Consumers Union. 1998. Fruits and vegetables: Nature's best protection. *Consumer Reports on Health* 10 (6):1-5.

Evans, G. 1989. The effect of chromium picolinate on insulin controlled parameters in humans. *International Journal of Biosocial and Medical Research* 11:163-80.

Fahey, T.D. and M.S. Pearl. The hormonal and perceptive effects of phosphatidylserine administration. *Biological Sport,* in press.

Fawcett, J., et al. 1996. The effect of oral vanadyl sulfate on body composition and performance in weight-training athletes. *International Journal of Sport Nutrition* 6:382-90.

Gastelu, D., and Hatfield, F. 1997. *Dynamic Nutrition for Maximum Performance.* Avery Publishing Group, Garden City Park, NY.

Grossman and Hart, *The Insulin Resistance Diet,* Cheryl R. Hart and Mary Kay Grossman, Lincolnwood, IL. Contemporary Books 2001

Haller, C., and Benowitz, N. 2000. Adverse cardiovascular and central nervous system events associated with dietary supplements containing ephedra alkaloids. *New England Journal of Medicine* 343:1833-38.

Hargreaves, M., et al. 1996. Effect of fluid ingestion on muscle metabolism during prolonged exercise. *Journal of Applied Physiology* 80:363-66.

Harris, R., et al. 1992. Elevation of creatine in resting and exercised muscle on normal subjects by creatine supplementation. *Clinical Science* 83:367-74.

Hawley, J., and Burke, L. 1998. *Peak Performance: Training and Nutritional Strategies for Sport.* St. Leonards, NSW: Allen and Unwin Australia.

Heath, E., et al. 1993. Effect of nicotinic acid on respiratory exchange ratio and substrate levels during exercise. *Medicine and Science in Sport and Exercise* 25:1018-23.

Hogervorst, E., et al. 1999. Caffeine improves cognitive performance after strenuous physical exercise. *International Journal of Sports Medicine* 20:354-60.

Ivy, J. and Portman, R. 2004. *Nutrient Timing: The Future of Sports Nutrition.* Basic Health Publications, Inc. North Bergen, NJ.

Jenkins, D.J., et al., "Nibbling Versus Gorging: Metabolic Advantages of Increased Meal Frequency," *New England Journal of Medicine.* 321.14 (1989): 929-934.

Kalman, D., et al. 1999. The effects of pyruvate supplementation on body composition in overweight individuals. *Nutrition* 15:337-40.

Kingsbury, K. J., et al. 1998. Contrasting plasma free amino acid patterns in elite athletes. *British Journal of Sports Medicine* 32:25-32.

Kreider, R., et al. 1992. Effects of phosphate loading on metabolic and myocardial responses to maximal and endurance exercise. *International Journal of Sport Nutrition* 2:20-47.

Kriketos, A., et al. 1999. Hydroxycitric acid does not affect energy expenditure and substrate oxidation in adult males in a post-absorptive state. *International Journal of Obesity and Related Metabolic Disorders* 23:867-73.

Krotkiewski, M., et al. 1982. Zinc and muscle strength and endurance. *Acta Physiologica Scandinavica* 116:309-11.

Lemon, P., et al. 1992. Protein requirements and muscle mass/strength changes during intensive training in novice bodybuilders. *Journal of Applied Physiology* 73:767-75.

Lemon, P. W. 1998. Effects of exercise on dietary protein requirements. *International Journal of Sports Nutrition,* 8:426-47.

Lukaski, H. 2001. Magnesium, zinc, and chromium nutrition and athletic performance. *Canadian Journal of Applied Physiology* 26:S13-22.

Lukaszuk, J., et al. 2002. Effect of creatine supplementation and lactoovovegetarian diet on muscle creatine concentration. *International Journal of Sport Nutrition and Exercise Metabolism* 12:336-48.

Matson, L., and Tran, Z. V. 1993. Effects of sodium bicarbonate ingestion on anaerobic performance: A meta- analytic review. *International Journal of Sports Nutrition* 3:2-28.

McNaughton, L., and Thompson, D. 2001. Acute versus chronic sodium bicarbonate ingestion and anaerobic work and power output. *Journal of Sports Medicine and Physical Fitness* 41:456-62.

McNaughton, L., et al. 1999. Inosine supplementation has no effect on aerobic or anaerobic cycling performance. *International Journal of Sport Nutrition* 9:333-44.

Mittleman, K.D., et al. 1998. Branched-chain amino acids prolong exercise during heat stress in mean and women. *Medicine and Science in Sports and Exercise* 30:83-91.

Morgan, S., et al. 1997. A low-fat diet supplemented with monounsaturated fat results in less HDL-C lowering than a very low-fat diet. *Journal of the American Dietetic Association* 97:151-56.

Naghii, M. JR. 1999. The significance of dietary boron, with particular reference to athletes. *Nutrition and Health* 13:31-37.

National Academy of Sciences. Institute of Medicine, Food and Nutrition Board. 1999. *Dietary Reference Intakes for Calcium, Phosphorus, Magnesium, Vitamin D, and Fluoride.* Washington, DC: National Academy Press.

National Academy of Sciences. 2002. *Dietary Reference Intakes for Energy, Carbohydrates, Fiber, Fat, Protein and Amino Acids (Macronutrients).* Washington, DC: National Academies Press.

Newsholme, E., and Blomstrand, E. 1996. The plasma level of some amino acids and physical and mental fatigue. *Experientia* 52:413-15.

Nielsen, F. 1992. Facts and fallacies about boron. *Nutrition Today* 27:6-12.

Nissen, S., et al. 1996. Effect of leucine metabolite B-hydroxy-B-methylbutyrate on muscle metabolism during resistance exercise training. *Journal of Applied Physiology* 81:2095-2104.

Parry-Billings, M., et al. 1992. Plasma amino acid concentrations in the overtraining dyndrome: Possible effects on the immune system. *Medicine and Science in Sports and Exercise* 24:1353-58.

Pieper, J. 2002. Understanding niacin formulations. *American Journal of Management Care* 8:5308-14.

Preen, D., et al. 2003. Creatine supplementation: A comparison of loading and maintenance protocols on creatine uptake by human skeletal muscle. *International Journal of Sport Nutrition and Metabolism* 13:97-111.

Preen, D., et al. 2001. Effect of creatine loading on long-term sprint exercise performance and metabolism. *Medicine and Science in Sports and Exercise* 33:814-21.

Saltzman, E. and Roberts, S.B. 1995. The role of energy expenditure in energy regulation. *Nutr. Rev* 53 (8):209-220.

Staton, W. 1951. The influence of soya lecithin on muscular strength. *Research Quarterly* 22:201-207.

Svensson, M., et al. 1999. Effect of Q10 supplementation on tissue Q10 levels and adenine nucleotide catabolism during high-intensity exercise. *International Journal of Sport Nutrition* 9:166-80.

Tarnopolsky, M., and Cupido, C. 2000. Caffeine potentiates low frequency skeletal muscle force in habitual and nonhabitual caffeine consumers. *Journal of Applied Physiology* 89:1719-24.

Tipton, K.D., and Wolfe, R.R. 1998. Exercise-induced changes in protein metabolism. *Acta Physiologica Scandinavica* 162:377-87.

Trappe, S., eta al. 1994. The effect of L-carnitine supplementation on performance during interval swimming. *International Journal of Sports Medicine* 15:181-85.

Verboeket-van de Venne, W.P., et al. "Influence of the Feeding Frequency on Nutrient Utilization in Man: Consequences for Energy Metabolism," *European Journal of Clinical Nutrition.* 45.3 (1991): 161-169.

Wagenmakers, A. 2000. Amino acid metabolism in exercise. In *Nutrition in Sport,* ed. R.J. Maughan. Oxford: Blackwell Science.

Wagner, D.R. 1999. Hyperhydrating with glycerol. *Journal of the American Dietetic Association* 99:207-12.

Warber, J., et al. 2000. The effects of choline supplementation on physical performance. *International Journal of Sport Nutrition and Exercise Metabolism* 10:170-81.

Wesson, M., et al. 1988. Effects of oral administration of aspartic salts on the endurance capacity of trained athletes. *Research Quarterly for Exercise and Sport* 59:234-39.

Weston, S., et al. 1997. Does exogenous coenzyme Q10 affect aerobic capacity in endurance athletes? *International Journal of Sport Nutrition* 7:197-206.

Williams. Nutrition for Health, Exercise, and Sport, 2002. Williams, M. H. 1999. Facts and fallacies of purported ergogenic amino acid supplements. *Clinics in Sports Medicine* 18:633-49.

Zambell, K., et al. 2001. Conjugated linoleic acid supplementation in humans: Effects on fatty acid and glycerol kinetics, *Lipids* 36:767-72.